Staving Off Disaster

Staving Off Disaster

§

Part 1: A Journey in Biblical Fasting A Guide for Christians in Times of Crisis

Gregory E. Von Tobel

Mahanaim Creek Publishers LLC
Woodinville, Washington

ISBN-13: 9781536890600

ISBN-10: 153689060X

Library of Congress Control Number: 2016912827
CreateSpace Independent Publishing Platform
North Charleston, South Carolina

As firstfruits, this book is dedicated to my Lord and Savior, Jesus Christ, who picked me up from the muck and the mire of life and gave me eternal salvation, a new life, a new purpose, and a new set of clothes.

To Him and Him alone, all glory and honor be bestowed!

Contents

Foreword

Staving Off Disaster is a must-read for every Christian, especially those on the front lines of ministry. Greg Von Tobel addresses the biblical discipline of fasting and brings practical application through his personal life journey with this spiritual discipline.

As chairman of the board of Prisoners For Christ Outreach Ministries, I have ministered together with Greg for more than twenty years in the jails, prisons, and juvenile institutions across Washington State, throughout the United States, and internationally. I've seen him in the Master's refining fire more than once. I'm amazed at his wisdom, discernment, focus, strength, and godliness in the innumerable situations I've witnessed. The Lord is glorified in him and through him.

Today, too many Christians are not experiencing victory in Christ—divorce, immorality, and substance abuse are major concerns in the Christian community. Other *lesser* issues like envy, anger, rebellion, laziness, and irresponsibility also seem to tie the hands of believers, rendering them ineffective for the Gospel. Then there are those with issues of worry, depression, anxiety, and fear. Our nation, including our churches, is being battered with the message that homosexual and transgender behavior is normal and should be accepted without question. This onslaught is touching the entire fabric of the Christian community. We ask what is missing that seems to be rendering the Christian powerless and stymied. We read our Bibles, we pray, and we seek counseling, but it seems something is missing—something to catalyze the power of Christ in our lives.

I've always believed that the Bible has the answer to every problem and that God is personally concerned for His children. Seeing sincere Christians falling short of God's plan for their lives is quite painful. There is an answer to these issues. Greg addresses these issues and more in his book, *Staving Off Disaster*.

This book reveals Greg's armor—his calm in the storm. It's his great dependency on and faith in Jesus Christ, but even further, it's his commitment to fasting and prayer that makes Greg the man he is today. Greg is the founder and leader of an international prison ministry that continues to grow and is devoid of the issues that plague so many other ministries—debt, dysfunction, division, scandal, and even an abandonment of the faith. His marriage is strong. His testimony is sound. He knows whereof he speaks. His life and ministry bespeak of a mature man of God, the kind of person every Christian wants to be but where far too many fall short.

Read *Staving Off Disaster*, and see how God works in ordinary individuals' lives through the largely ignored biblical discipline of fasting. Apply these truths to your own life—Greg has written a simple plan of action for how you can get started. Behold how God works through you to win the victory to *Stave Off Disaster*.

Dr. Robert F. "Bob" Jordan
Chairman, Prisoners For Christ Outreach Ministries
International Group Leader

Preface

BELIEVERS AROUND THE world are facing unbelievable struggles and trials of epic proportion. You may be one who is walking through the fire right now. Life is difficult at best. However the Bible states, "Consider it pure joy, my brothers, whenever you face trials of many kinds" (James 1:2). The question that needs to be asked and answered is, how do you face trials with joy in your heart? It is beyond understanding. However, as I have matured in Christ, I have experienced five life-changing events that have radically altered the course of my life—so much so that when trials do come my way, I am able to handle them much differently than the old man of flesh would have.

The first life experience for me was in 1982 when Christ came into my life in a powerful way. My life was transformed in a heartbeat. It has never been the same since that moment in time. Many of my old habits and mannerisms dropped off immediately, while others took years of honing and pruning by the Holy Spirit. I am a better man for what Christ has done through me through His life-changing message of the Gospel.

The second life experience that radically changed my life occurred in 1984 when I was dragged off, kicking and screaming, to my first prison ministry experience. I was a stockbroker at the time and had absolutely no desire to sacrifice my time going into prison. Fast-forward six years later to 1990: I had left my job as a stockbroker to work in the prisons as a full-time missionary. Prison ministry has revolutionized my Christian walk. It is a true gift from God. I am incredibly blessed by my interaction with the inmates, and I want to pass that blessing on to others...but they don't want it. If the Christian world understood what a gift it is to go into the jails and prisons, I would have crowds—no mobs—every morning and evening pounding at my door yelling, "Let me go too!" Sadly, most people shrug and look disinterested when they are invited to go. They turn and walk away. I want to grab them, shake them, and say, "You don't know what you are giving up."

The third life experience occurred in the late-1980s after my conversion experience, when I finally learned the biblical message on tithing. Before that time, I was stingy. I didn't give. The message of tithing had to be pounded into me regularly. Today my wife, Rhonda, and I are givers. Giving has radically changed our lives. I can't imagine today what my life would be if we didn't give. I am truly blessed in life because of the discipline of giving. Because of that faithfulness, God has poured back into our lives more than I could have ever imagined.

The fourth life experience that radically changed my life occurred in 1999 when Rhonda and I went on our first mission trip to India. Even as I was maturing in my walk of faith, I vehemently did not want to go. I gave five major reasons why we shouldn't go on that trip. My wife agreed with me, but she said, "We really should at least pray about it." Within ten days, all five major reasons had vanished, and so, we went to India. That trip turned our lives upside down.

Stepping out of our bubble here in the Northwest and seeing what God was doing in the poorest parts of India radically changed our lives. It changed our lives to such an extent that we soon experienced the next level of growth in prison ministry by taking regular, short-term, international prison ministry trips. Thirty-eight trips later, the awe is still there! However, when I ask people to go on mission trips, I hear so many different excuses as to why people can't go. Again, I want to grab them and shake them and say, "You don't know what you are giving up." If Christians would just rise above their life of *stuff* and step out of their comfort zones, I would have a mob pounding down my door yelling, "Let me go with you!"

The fifth and last life experience that has radically changed my life is understanding the power of fasting—thus the reason for writing this book.

Again, much like prison ministry and going on that first mission trip, I had no interest in the discipline of fasting. However, as the years marched on, the power of the Holy Spirit helped me to realize that fasting is such a misunderstood discipline in our churches today. It is looked upon as the black sheep of spiritual disciplines. For many years, I have often sat across the table from people who have openly wept over trials in their lives. I would then ask a simple question: "Have you ever fasted for this particular situation?" After a long, awkward pause, I would discover they had never fasted in their Christian walk—nor would they even know how to begin.

This book is for all the Christians who have never fasted or who don't even know how to begin. I come to you with tears, begging you to read and understand the biblical principles of fasting found in this book. Understand the promises in Isaiah 58, which are given to one who fasts properly. Fasting is one of the most powerful spiritual tools we as believers have in our spiritual arsenals, yet for most of us, it is nothing more than a dust collector! It is rarely used by the average Christian. Pick this weapon up, and become a *radicalized* Christian for the cause of Christ.

Greg Von Tobel
President
Prisoners For Christ Outreach Ministries

Acknowledgments

I WANT TO acknowledge the extraordinary efforts of a few friends and co-laborers, without whose help this book would not be what it is today.

I would like to first and foremost thank my dear wife of thirty-nine years, Rhonda Von Tobel, who, with her signature smile, is my biggest fan and life partner. To the love of my life, thanks for reading, offering all of your suggestions, and giving sound advice in certain sticky parts of the book.

I would also like to thank my beta readers:

Nate Bean, board member of Prisoners For Christ (PFC), who, in spite of his hectic business schedule and international travels with PFC, found time to catch typos with his keen eye and to challenge me to rephrase things for readability.

Peyton Burkhart, editor of PFC's national inmate newspaper, *Yard Out*, for really great last-minute suggestions.

Monte Cline, for the awesome work on the video for the Kickstarter campaign.

Frank "Eagle Eye" Follansbee, who applied his attention for detail to reviewing the Bible studies in the appendix.

Bob Jordan, my closest confidant, friend, and Prisoners For Christ board chairman, who gave valuable insight into this book and also wrote the foreword.

Jill Payne-Holman, senior vice president of finance for Prisoners For Christ, who took it upon herself to complete the first round of editing. Without her self-sacrificing time spent editing, this book would be in a round file collecting dust. Thank you, Jill, for the hours of reading, editing, and meetings with the boss.

My friend Ray Ruppert, with his incredible eye for thoroughness in formatting and footnoting, as well as his ability to challenge me on some of my conclusions—a huge thank you.

In addition to the board members of PFC mentioned above, my appreciation goes to the rest of the board of directors who so diligently serve Prisoners For Christ with their time and talents—Dave Holmes, Bob Rogers, and Don Szolomayer.

Cautionary Notes from the Author

PLEASE UNDERSTAND THAT fasting for any length of time can be harmful to your body. Fasting is not for everyone. The rule of thumb—consult your medical practitioner before embarking on fasting, and know your body! Use godly discernment to determine if God is calling you to *any* length of a fast. Consult with your spouse, your pastor, your accountability partners, and especially your physician about your desire to fast. This book was written solely from a spiritual perspective and is based on the author's personal experience.

Those who should *not* fast include those suffering with life-threatening diseases, such as diabetes or cancer; those on chemo or radiation; those preparing for surgery; pregnant or nursing moms; children; those with compromised immune systems; those with mental health issues; and those who have struggled with eating disorders.

Those who should be highly *cautioned* when considering fasting are the elderly, those on prescription drug medications, or those whose daily routine includes physical exertion of their bodies. This is not meant to be an exhaustive list. If you choose to go forward with fasting, you should consult with your medical practitioner before embarking on that journey. Once into a fast, if your body is telling you something, seek immediate medical assistance.

For those Christians who are active on the Internet, please be aware of the source of the material you are reading. Many false religions use fasting as well; don't be fooled by their websites. Others sites will try to sell you a weight-loss program, so remember that true spiritual fasting has nothing to do with losing weight.

UNIT 1

The Beginning

CHAPTER 1

The Presidential Election That Changed My Spiritual Life

In 1982, I was involved in a war...a spiritual war...a war for the destiny of my soul. Accepting the Christian faith did not come easily for me. It took a powerful encounter with God to snatch my soul from the enemy. I lost my old life—a self-centered, miserable existence of worldly ambition. I gained a new heart through the redemptive power of Jesus Christ. I lost—but I won! Never would I have imagined what lay ahead of me in my new life. Never would I have planned the path I would travel. Never would I have foreseen the blessings—or the gut-wrenching trials—that I would experience. This book is about one such trial. This is my story.

7:30 a.m.—Tuesday, November 7, 2000—Election Day

It was a typical, rain-soaked day in the Pacific Northwest. I awoke as I had always done, early in the morning, for an extended period of quiet time before the Lord. Looking out the window, I noticed the dark, gray clouds that I was so accustomed to seeing. Because daylight savings time had come and gone, the days were becoming shorter and shorter, causing the drab grayness that is so typical during the winter months. The Northwest gets rain the way the Midwest gets snow: rain that drizzles, rain that blows, rain that flies sideways. Gray days abound. For some, it is too much. They gut it out for a season or two only to return from whence they came.

Although I didn't know it, this day was to be a difficult one. It would be a day that would change my spiritual life for the remaining years of my life. It would also be a day that would wear on into midnight and early into the morning of the next day. As far as I knew, that day would present the normal challenges of running a ministry. It would be a routine day, or so I thought. However, it turned out to be all but routine!

In the late 1990s the Washington State Department of Corrections was in an expansion mode, in which a number of new prisons were to be built in order to implement the "get tough on crime" laws mandated by our legislature. One of those prisons was Stafford Creek Correctional Center, located in the Aberdeen/Hoquiam area of southwest Washington. When I received a call from the new program manager requesting that Prisoners For Christ (PFC) start a new church service at the institution, I was more than happy to take a look at potential opportunities to open up a new outreach to this prison.

Back in the early years, the ministry primarily focused on sending volunteers to prisons and jails within an hour's drive of the Seattle metropolitan area. Stafford Creek posed a new set of problems, as it was a three-hour drive from our core volunteer base in Seattle.

After several weeks of negotiations with the chaplain and program director, it was agreed upon that PFC would conduct services at Stafford Creek on Tuesday nights. The three-hour drive, coupled with a midweek service, was more than most of our Seattle-based volunteers could handle. After much discussion with my wife, Rhonda, we agreed that I would start the team, with the idea of recruiting volunteers from the Aberdeen area. Within six months of the start-up, a commitment that Rhonda and I were willing to make, I would slowly turn the leadership reins over to the locals.

In order to arrive at the agreed upon time at Stafford Creek Correctional Center, I needed to leave the PFC offices in Kirkland at three o'clock in the afternoon. That day, November 7, it rained all day. It didn't let up as the day progressed; in fact, it intensified. I didn't look forward to the drive—not only because the rain was blowing sideways but also because I was driving an older diesel Suburban, which I had nicknamed Bubba.

Bubba was donated to the ministry by some dear friends who knew I needed a reliable vehicle to travel around to different institutions.

Bubba was reliable but was showing its age. The passenger-side window would no longer roll down, there was a hydraulic leak on the driver's-side floor, and worst of all, it had no working radio. Because it was old, it drove like a tank and was not a comfortable ride for long trips. Driving rain and a three-hour ride with no radio made for a long, tedious drive. But I loved Bubba, and Bubba loved me! I could always count on Bubba starting and taking me where I needed to go. Reliable amenities—not so much!

The drive to Stafford Creek that day was particularly long as I had not slept much the night before. Between rain pelting the windshield and my needing toothpicks to keep my eyes open, I struggled to keep Bubba between the lines on the road.

I always look forward to the fall, as it is one of my favorite seasons in the Northwest. However, because of the excess of rain that year, the fall colors were not as vibrant as in years past. The scenery was particularly drab with muted colors.

After stopping for a light dinner in Aberdeen, I arrived at the prison at six thirty that evening, just in time to meet my new team of volunteers. Once cleared by the correctional staff, the PFC team had to walk through many other clearance doors in order to arrive at the chapel. It took about ten minutes of walking outside to get to the all-purpose room where we would hold chapel that evening. The cold, chilling rain cut into our faces as we made the trek. Once inside the chapel, we began setting up for the church service. The volunteers were all new and had only attended PFC church services a couple of times. For this reason, I conducted the entire service from start to finish in order to model how the new volunteers should run the church services once I turned the reins of leadership over to them.

The inmates always love to sing. For that reason we would typically open with thirty to forty minutes of worship songs. Not having any natural musical ability myself, I was glad to have a couple of the inmates, who were preapproved by staff, to lead worship and take over this part of the church service. We quickly moved into a time of testimony sharing by the inmates, followed by preaching and then the altar call. The strange thing about that evening was that I lost all track of time. It was unusual to have extra time, but that evening we had about twenty-five extra minutes of free time to fill. I prayed that the Holy Spirit would lead me in how best to fill that twenty-five-minute void.

"OK, men, listen up. We are going to do something different tonight. I want you to gather into groups of five or six." With about sixty men in the group, I quickly estimated we would have about ten groups.

"What is today?"

"Tuesday!" shouted one inmate, while others around the room snickered.

"That's right. It is Tuesday, but what is the importance of *this* Tuesday?"

"It's Election Day," shouted another inmate.

"Very good, we have a smart crowd tonight. You are a smarter group than you look." More snickers. "That is absolutely correct. It is Election Day, and I have already voted. This is a very important election for this country—very important. Do you understand what I mean?"

Lots of heads nodded.

"Now listen to me and listen closely. I don't care what political party you are affiliated with. What I do care about is that today, Tuesday, November 7, is Election Day, and I want all of you to circle up and lift your prayers to the Lord Almighty, *standing in the gap* for this country. Pray that God would not withdraw His hand from America and that we would be able to continue to live under His favor.

"Do you understand my instructions? Either sit or kneel at your chair. We have twenty-five minutes before we leave, so let's do business with God tonight."

For the next twenty-five minutes, as I walked and stood by each group, I was moved to tears. In society's eyes, these men were the throwaways of our nation. They had done much wrong, and they'd had many of their freedoms—including the right to vote—taken away because of their transgressions. However, you would never have known that they were in prison if you had heard their cries to God. They were travailing in prayer for this country. Their sweet and humble pleas often moved me to tears during our short time together. In their small groups, I heard many of these inmates pray, "If my people, who are called by my name, will humble themselves and pray and seek my face and turn from their wicked ways, then will I hear from heaven and will forgive their sin and will heal their land" (2 Chronicles 7:14).

I have never participated in exit polling; I don't believe in exit polling. However, after listening to their prayers, I would have had to conclude that the majority of these sixty men were Republicans. This surprised me...no, it shocked me!

As we left the chapel for our ten-minute walk back to the main building, I was happy to see that the rain had stopped. During this time, I intentionally kept my mouth shut and remained silent. I was waiting.

It only took about five seconds out the door before one of our volunteers said, "Did you hear some of their prayers?"

"Yes, I did. Wasn't that awesome?" I replied.

"I really wasn't expecting that!" exclaimed another volunteer. "The Holy Spirit was all over those men."

As we left the institution, I was looking for my tried-and-true friend, Bubba. There he was, just sitting patiently in the now-vacant, lonely, prison parking lot. I wondered if this would be the day Bubba would forsake me and leave me destitute on a long, dark road in Washington State. As I put the key in the ignition, Bubba's diesel engine roared to life. I patted the dashboard as a sign of affection.

"Thank you, Jesus, and you too, Bubba."

By the time I left the institution, it was already nine thirty. This would put me home around twelve thirty the following morning. Having no radio in Bubba prevented me from tuning in to the election results and made for an extremely boring ride home. I remember those late-night trips back from Stafford Creek—nothing short of arduous.

Day One—12:30 a.m.—Wednesday, November 8, 2000

My home, my home, my sanctuary! I was glad to peel myself out of Bubba's front seat. Once again I patted the dashboard as one would pat man's best friend. "Good job, Bubba. Nicely done. I'm going to bed, so I'll see you tomorrow."

As I strolled into our living room, I noticed the lights were on, which was unusual, as Rhonda normally would already have been in bed. However, this evening she was up waiting for me. "What are you doing up so late, honey?"

"Watching the election results."

"Really! Did Bush win?"

"Nobody knows yet. It's still up in the air."

"Really! What do you mean 'still up in the air'? Normally, elections are called by six o'clock in the evening, West Coast time."

"A couple of the networks are calling Gore the winner!"

"Really!"

"However they have since rescinded that."

"Really!"

"The results are too close to call in Florida, Oregon, and New Mexico."

"Really!"

"It's been reported that Gore is about to call Bush and concede."

"Really!"

"Will you stop saying 'really'? I'm going to bed. Good night."

Normally, after a three-hour drive from Stafford Creek, I would have immediately crawled into bed and been fast asleep before my head hit the pillow—but not that evening. I was glued to the TV. It was as if we were in for a good, old-fashioned, Rocky Balboa street fight, and I wasn't going to miss it. Back and forth I toggled between channels, one pundit to another pundit, waiting, waiting, and more waiting.

Breaking news on one channel stated that Mr. Gore had called Mr. Bush and taken his concession off the table. "Enough of this!" I thought. "I'm going to bed. I can barely keep my eyes open." Confident the election would be over by morning, I headed upstairs as I mumbled something under my breath about the press being at fault for the early election results.

As I fell asleep, I fully expected to hear the results in the morning. Little did I know...

CHAPTER 2

§

The Morning After

9:00 a.m.—Wednesday, November 8, 2000

After a late night of ministry, I often would take the liberty of sleeping in the next morning. I awoke around nine o'clock after a deep, wonderful sleep. I instantly shot up out of bed and began looking for Rhonda. "Who's our next president?"

With a strange look on her face, she said, "No winner."

"What?"

"No winner!"

"What do you mean 'no winner'?"

Sigh. "No winner." A comical look of indignation shot across her face as if to say, "Why do I have to tell you everything three different times?"

"Are you yanking my chain?"

"Look!" she said as she pointed to the television in our bedroom.

Within a nanosecond, I was transfixed by the TV. I couldn't understand what was happening and didn't understand how there could be no winner. This had never happened before! Mr. Bush had 245 electoral votes, and Mr. Gore had 255. Both candidates were far from the 270 electoral votes needed to be declared the next president. The news channels were awash with the news that three states were too close to call: Florida, Oregon, and New Mexico. All eyes were fixed on Florida with its twenty-five electoral votes.

I began my daily routine, all the while keeping my eyes fixated on the newscasts. I threw on sweats and headed downstairs to my favorite quiet-time chair.

I was quite perplexed regarding the outcome of the election and felt a quickening in my spirit—a somberness I had never experienced before. Alone with the Lord, I felt the Holy Ghost–spiritual goose bumps start slowly at the tips of my toes and slowly travel to the back of my neck. I meditated on the happenings of the election. I immediately felt the presence of the Lord envelope me as I stepped into deep, fervent prayer. The Spirit brought to mind the sweet and heartfelt prayers for our country that the inmates had offered up the night before. I flashed back immediately to the humble prayers of the inmates—those broken and throwaway men, coming before the throne of the Almighty on behalf of this country's future—the prayers of the repentant flooding the throne of the Most High.

The vision seemed to last for an eternity, but it was really just a few minutes. Right before my very eyes, I saw *rejects* of our society being transformed into great warriors for the Lord, reaching to the ceiling nine feet tall, spiritual giants committed to prayer.

Then it happened. I heard it. "Will you *stand in the gap* for this country?" Silence on my part. My words from the night before came flooding back to me, quickly reminding me that I had used the exact same words, "*stand in the gap* for this country," which the still, small voice was now repeating back to me. In silence I pondered the strangeness of the question.

I was impressed to immediately look the verse up in my Bible: "I looked for a man among them who would build up the wall and stand before me in the gap on behalf of the land so I would not have to destroy it, but I found none" (Ezekiel 22:30).

"Will you *stand in the gap*, Greg?" Silence on my part.

"Will you *stand in the gap*, Greg?" I heard the question a third time. "Yes, Lord! But what does that mean? Help me! I don't know what that means or what You want."

Little did I know that those two words, "Yes, Lord," would change my spiritual life forever! I would, in a sense, be ruined for life...in a good way.

"Will you pray and fast until the election is over?"

"Yes, Lord!" Silence, as if the metal prison gate had slammed shut in its finality—a deafening silence.

As quickly as it had occurred, it was over.

Hmmm…what was that all about? I wondered. Well, apparently I had just committed to pray and fast until the election was over. I knew I could fast until six o'clock on Wednesday evening, no problem. I did the math. With some quick calculations, I figured I could go without two meals. I mentally figured the election would be over by the time I returned home to watch the world news that night. Making it to six o'clock would be no big deal. Slam dunk!

Little did I know!

11:00 a.m.—Wednesday, November 8, 2000

Once again I was driving to work in Bubba, my diesel friend with no radio. I found myself knee-deep in work at the ministry and was virtually on the "dark side of the moon," with little to no information as to the nation's plight. Around noon I was tempted by the enemy to break my fast and go wrap my hands around a big, fat, juicy Big Mac at Mickey D's. The temptation was fierce. I felt like I was losing the battle. Philippians 4:13 was brought to mind: "I can do everything through him who gives me strength." I gutted it out. Because the battle to resist a burger was so fierce, I knew something was up in the heavenlies, so I dug in my heels.

Had it not been for the memories that flooded my mind, I could have very easily folded and given up. But recalling the inmates at Stafford Creek, with their simple but humble prayers, and reflecting on how the presence of the Lord had fallen over me several hours earlier, I gutted it out. At that point I had told no one, not even my wife, about the commitment I had made to pray and fast till the election was over.

The work day was incredibly insane. Because of the hectic nature of the day, I was able to keep my mind occupied. I rushed home to catch the six o'clock world news. Waiting for me was a plate of vegetarian spaghetti, one of my favorite dishes! Rhonda makes it especially for me!

I rushed by everyone and clicked on the news.

"Hello!"

"Hi, honey."

"Come eat."

"Who won the election?"

"No one yet."

Absolutely horrified by her answer, I tuned everything out for the next fifteen minutes. I must have turned twelve shades of deathly pale green. Rhonda began to drill me with questions as to why I was so agitated. I proceeded to tell her and my father, who had been living with us since the death of my mom, about the strange conversation I'd had with the Lord that morning...about how I had committed to pray and fast until the election was resolved. They both just stopped and stared at me in disbelief. And once again I was faced with silence...awkward, deafening silence!

What Have I Done?

Day Two—9:00 a.m.—Thursday, November 9, 2000

I found myself very much distracted with my mind racing and jumping from topic to topic. On the way to work, I decided to swing by the local Safeway store and pick up some juice to tide me over for another day of fasting, something I hadn't done on the first day. I had made a commitment in my mind to stay the course. Juice was the only idea I had as to how I might make it through the day without falling over and curling up into fetal position. Little did I know that the juice aisle of the local Safeway store would become my new best friend by the end of the fast. I would end up spending countless hours perusing the different kinds of juices. I was quite amazed at the different combinations of juices that man has conjured up.

Up to that point, I had only fasted a total of five days in my entire Christian walk, with only two of those days being consecutive. I once again did the math and figured I could do a three-day fast. The thought of this being a slam dunk had all but faded into oblivion, but I really felt

13

pretty confident that I could at least power through today and tomorrow for a three-day fast.

§

At that time, I had been a Christian for eighteen years—not a new believer by any sense of the term, but then again, not a fully seasoned warrior either. Fasting was a foreign concept to me. I had heard of people fasting but had no formal teaching from the pulpit.

In America we have it all. We are a nation blessed by God. The downside to that prosperity is that whenever problems occur, we rely on our own problem-solving techniques and not on God's sovereignty. Fasting is a forgotten and ignored discipline that is rarely taught. Because America is so prosperous, we as a nation rarely find the need to fall prostrate before the Lord, praying for serious and life-threatening problems.

About nine months after the 2000 election, our country would suffer the most horrific attack on our homeland soil since Pearl Harbor: that was 9/11. Our churches would be flooded with people who had not seen the inside of a church for decades. Our country was on the verge of a revival, calling upon the Lord to renew our strength. Our country vowed to rebuild, and we did. However, we rebuilt in our own strength and not in the Lord's. It didn't take too long before our jammed churches started to empty out. Why? Because our prosperity was a distraction. Our prosperity became our god, our idol, once again. We were reliving the fate of the nation of Israel of the Old Testament, of coming to the Lord in their hour of need and falling away once that need had been filled.

Prosperity and fasting, for the most part, cannot coexist, or should I say, they have a great problem coexisting in the same world, which we will learn more about later in this book.

As founder and president of Prisoners For Christ for the past two decades, I have been blessed by the opportunity to travel the world, seeding the vision of taking the lifesaving message of Jesus Christ into some of the darkest and most remote prisons on the face of this earth. As of this writing, PFC has field offices in fourteen different countries. I have traveled the developing world in an attempt to train and equip the local pastorate to do prison ministry. In the process, I have found several principles to be in effect.

First and foremost, our international counterparts have very little in material possessions, but they have far surpassed us here in America with their faith walk and their prayer life. Here in America, we have much in material possessions; however, our prayer life and our faith walk pale in comparison to those who live their lives in other countries. I am often asked, who is more blessed? My answer is always the same: "They are!" These men and women of God are my heroes. These pastors have a daily walk with the Lord. It is powerful and intimate, the likes of which our American brothers and sisters would only dream of having.

Second, our pastoral counterparts understand the power that comes from regular, spiritual fasts. I have heard many reports from our affiliates of having a protracted time of fasting. Why do they understand it and we don't? One word: distractions. Our wealth has become a distraction. It causes us to lose focus on what truly matters in life. With more wealth comes more stuff, with more stuff comes more distractions, and with more distractions comes less focus on spiritual things. The distractions of maintenance and breakdowns, the mental capacity to deal with contracts—all of these add to the complexity of life.

Is it sinful to be wealthy? Maybe, maybe not. Where are your priorities? Is your wealth an idol? Are you hoarding your wealth for self-consumption, or are you using it to build up the kingdom of God? Has it consumed your thinking to the point where it crowds out all other thinking of heavenly values? Does the fear of never having enough consume your thoughts? With less stuff, our pastoral counterparts on the other side of the world have more time to focus on their need for a fruitful prayer life, as well as their need to fast for their daily provisions, which we take for granted.

§

By midmorning of day two, I started to feel dizzy and light-headed—a new feeling for me. So I did the only thing I knew to do—I pounded down some juice. I was unable to concentrate as I felt nauseated. I had a headache that was mind-numbing. Some believe the fasting headache is due to blood sugar fluctuations or the body burning ketones for fuel, while others believe it is due to the body releasing toxins. Temptation was all around me—serious temptation—and thoughts of failure wrapped me in their wings. I fought, but the struggle was like never before. I sensed there was an immense spiritual battle taking place in the heavenlies.

The same pattern played out that day that had occurred on the previous one. I turned off the computer and crawled into Bubba for the long, silent drive home. As I walked into the house, I saw that Rhonda and Dad were glued to the television. There was silence in the room. This was not a good sign. They both stared at me with a look that sent shivers up my spine.

"You've got to be kidding me! Just count the ballots and call the election!" I said with no grace in my voice.

As we were getting ready for bed, Rhonda said, "Well?"

"Well, what?"

"How long are you going to do this? I am concerned and so is Dad."

"Honey, all I know for sure is I agreed to fast until the election is over. If this is truly from the Lord, which I totally believe it is at this point, He and He alone will sustain me. What's more, the election will be over by Friday. These idiots are not going to allow the election to go over the weekend. No way! It ain't going to happen. That would be political suicide. Trust me! On Friday, you, Dad, and I will go out for a big, fat, juicy burger. Trust me!"

Friday came and went. I could not believe they were going to carry this over the weekend. I settled into the reality that I was going to have to power through the weekend, and that by Monday evening at six o'clock, during the world news, I would be able to end my fast. I had a new goal: two more days. I could get to Monday night. There would be political posturing over the weekend. There would be many closed-door meetings, and there would be a deal cut by Monday at six. I was more than confident.

Day Four—8:30 a.m.—Saturday, November 11, 2000

Four days into the fast, and I was moping around the house like a spoiled brat. I was secretly embarrassed by my own thought life. I had a number of items on my "honey-do" list that I needed to catch up on, but in a split second I made the decision that Saturday would be a stay-in-pajamas day. I lay on the couch all day in my comfortable sweats.

As I flipped channels on the TV, I soon discovered that it was Veterans Day. I watched some of the old film clips of World War II and the Korean and Vietnam Wars. When I was seventeen, the government eliminated the draft, thus eliminating any possible chances of my going to Vietnam. This Veterans Day, I felt regret that I had never had a chance to serve my country like my father, uncles, or aunt. Back during World War II, my dad, along with his two brothers and their one sister, served in the military. All of them were from Peoria, Illinois (my hometown), and they all served at the same time: my dad and Aunt Betty in the marines, and my uncles, John and Paul, in the army. It was a big deal back then to have four siblings from the same family serving at one time.

In a very strange and unorthodox way, it struck me that I could very well be serving my country in a most powerful spiritual way. I settled into a comfortable position on the sofa to have a much-needed mental "veg" day.

Days five, six, seven, and eight were all incredibly painful days, both physically and mentally. It was the same old routine every day. In the morning I jumped into Bubba, went to the local Safeway store, grabbed several bottles of juice, and rushed in silence to work. The dizziness was fading away except for the times that I forgot to hydrate my body, and then it came roaring back with a vengeance.

Each evening I would rush home to find both Rhonda and Dad sitting in silence glued to the TV. Their silence told me everything. I came to the point that I didn't even ask anymore. I just bypassed the TV and went directly to the kitchen to see what kind of juice I would have for dinner. I internally grumbled and resented that I had ever made a commitment to the Lord. I was having a pity party in one sense, and in the other sense, I was quite frankly amazed that it had already been eight days without solid food. Never would I have imagined that I would be fasting for eight days straight, or that this could have even been possible. The Lord had been silent since the encounter the very first day—very silent. I pondered the silence in my heart, doubting. Did I really hear from the Lord?

The enemy uses doubt to render the saints ineffective for the cause of Christ. I knew this in my intellect, but the doubt was hard to shake. I had not done anything this radical since my conversion experience, except for quitting my job and going into full-time prison ministry. I knew I had to overcome the doubt. As 2 Corinthians 10:5 says, I needed to "take every thought captive." In reality, I doubted hearing from God correctly or, worse yet, listening to the wrong voice. I feared what damage I might be doing to my body. I worried about what others might be thinking of me. I doubted; I feared; I worried.

I had become very insecure by this point, and I knew it. This is the type of thought pattern that plagued me in the beginning days of the fast. I needed some encouragement—some signs that I was doing what I had heard I was to do. But on the other hand, I didn't want to be the one that always needed a fleece filled with dew in order to take action.

CHAPTER 3

———— § ————

Heaven Came Down

Day Nine—Thursday, November 16, 2000

ON THAT DAY, when I arrived home from the office, I was greeted with an entirely different demeanor from Rhonda and Dad. They were smiling with funny smirks on their faces. I thought, "Yes…it is over! Hallelujah! Amen and amen!" At that point I didn't even care who had won the election; I just wanted to eat! I was about ready to say, "Let's go party. Let's eat. I'm treating."

Sensing this was about to fall out of my mouth, Rhonda took a long, protracted pause as she stopped me by saying, "There's a problem!"

"What kind of a problem?" I sternly asked. I didn't like the way she said it. It seemed as if she had been anticipating this moment for some time, almost in a very macabre way. Her tone of voice was just downright weird. Her smile sent me a message of victory; however, the twinkle in her eye sent me a conflicting message. I felt hope slipping through my fingers. Rhonda mumbled something as she took another bite of food.

"What's the problem?"

"Chad is the problem," she mumbled again.

"Chad who? Do you mean our son Chad? Who the heck is Chad? I have never heard anyone mention anything about Chad," I yelled.

Silence. Dad began to smile. It seemed as if Rhonda and Dad had been having some fun at my expense, waiting for me to come home that evening. I looked at Dad. "Chad who?" I said as I lowered my voice.

"You are asking the wrong question. Instead of asking 'Chad who?' you should be asking 'Chad what?' It seems as if Chad is pregnant!" declared Dad.

"Huhhhhhh…you guys are messing with me. This isn't funny."

At that point I looked at my dad, who was laughing so hard I was afraid he might start snorting his food through his nose. It was a Kodak moment—my eighty-plus-year-old dad laughing so hard he was about ready to bust a gut. I believe laughter is a gift from God, and this was one of those "God moments"—this picture of my wife and my dad laughing so hard they couldn't swallow their spaghetti. Rhonda was literally convulsing on the couch at the word picture from Dad about Chad being pregnant. That moment would be seared into my mind for eternity, even after Dad's death at the age of ninety-four. That moment was truly one of the many gifts God gave me through the fast.

For the next hour, I sat shell-shocked as I was educated on how the election officials were trying to count the special votes that had a hole in them without the piece of paper being fully detached from the ballot. The media aptly named it "the hanging chad." They also labeled it the "pregnant chad"—those ballots with a bloated paper punched but not severed. The newscasters had a field day over this one. I looked at both Rhonda and Dad. I must admit, I too had tears of laughter rolling down my face.

Trust Me

Day Twelve—Sunday, November 19, 2000

"Greg, do you know what Thursday is?" Rhonda asked me.

"I may not be the sharpest tool in the shed, but I do know what Thursday is" came my snarkiest of replies.

It was Sunday night before Thanksgiving when this dialogue occurred. I knew Thanksgiving was bearing down on me, bringing with it my favorite time of the year—as well as my favorite meal.

"Trust me! The powers that be will not let the election go through the Thanksgiving holiday weekend. It would be political suicide to do something as stupid as that. Trust me!" I began to choke on my words, having come to the realization that whenever I used those two words together, "trust me," I seemed to be sealing my fate of having the exact opposite occur.

Wednesday night, the eve of Thanksgiving, began a new conversation.

"Well?" My wife looked at me.

"Well, what?" I looked back.

"Are you going to eat Thanksgiving dinner?"

"Nope!"

"Maybe you should break the fast for that one meal and then start up the following day!"

"Nope!"

"What are you going to tell the family?"

"Whatever falls out of my mouth!"

Day Sixteen—2:00 p.m.—Thursday, November 23—Thanksgiving—Hors d'Oeuvres before the Meal

So much food was brought to our house that I was half-mad I'd agreed to have Thanksgiving dinner there. I mentally sulked. If I had been at someone else's house, at least I might have been able to feign illness and just not shown up at all, thus sidestepping the inquisition that I knew was coming.

After much avoidance of the issue and coming up with reasons why I was not indulging in appetizers, Rhonda piped up in a high-octave voice. "Tell them!" I couldn't believe she had said that! Why had she said that? Was she sensing in her spirit that I would not be able to divulge my "secret"? Silence fell over the room as all eyes shifted to me.

"Go ahead and tell them!" she repeated. In her way, she was trying her best to help me out, but I wanted to crawl into the nearest hole.

"Tell them what?" I pretended I had no idea what she was talking about.

Silence continued to dominate the room while everyone looked at me for some profound words.

"Everybody...listen up. Greg has an announcement to make!" Rhonda tried again.

"I have no announcement to make!" I insisted.

"Greg is fasting. He won't be having Thanksgiving dinner today because he is fasting until the election is over." Rhonda took matters into her own hands because the words didn't "fall out of my mouth" as I had told her they would the night before. For the next thirty minutes, in rapid-fire succession, I attempted to answer as many questions as I could. Just as I managed to answer one question, a different family member began drilling me with another. During this time, there were many jaw-drops and startled expressions as they quickly calculated on their fingers the number of days that had passed since I had eaten any solid food.

As is the custom in our home, I prayed over the food and asked the Lord to bless the meal, as well as my juice. I could hear many snickers around the room. The family felt sorry for me for about two seconds, and then it was a free-for-all of face-stuffing. Several made very deliberate remarks about how unusually good the food was this year as they gave me side glances, hoping to make eye contact. Several made references to the extra amount of food that there would be for leftovers.

Heaven Came Down

I can't remember the exact day or time, but somewhere between day fifteen and day twenty, about the halfway mark of the fast, I had a spiritual breakthrough. The fast was still hard, as I continued pounding down two glasses of juice at each meal, plus two extra glasses throughout the day as my midmorning and midafternoon snacks. However, I felt as if something was changing inside of me as I approached the halfway mark of the fast. Something truly was changing! I was changing! What had seemed important to me in the not-too-distant past now seemed much more trivial. My level of discernment increased. I wondered, could it be that my eyesight is changing as well—not my physical eyesight, but my spiritual eyesight? Am I starting to see with spiritual eyes?

I felt as if the angels of God were within my grasp as I started seeing with spiritual eyes. Never before, and only in subsequent fasts, have I ever felt this close to our Lord and Savior. Physically, my energy levels became much higher.

I remember one particular afternoon so clearly. I was driving home early, and dusk was falling. My physical eyes began seeing God's creation in a whole different way than I had ever seen or experienced before. I remember a glint of sunlight shining through the trees as I wound my way down Novelty Hill Road. It was as if I were in a 3-D movie. It was as if I could reach out and grab hold of God's creation. Things glistened; things shone like never before. I wondered if this was what the world looked like before the fall of man. This ranks as one of the most spectacular events in my life, and one I rarely talk about in public.

The tears started to slowly flow as I felt the presence of the Spirit all around me. He enveloped me to the core of my being. The Spirit had been silent since the very first day of the fast when I had said, "Yes, Lord." That silence had fed my ongoing self-doubt. But now, I felt His presence all over me. I wept uncontrollably as I felt His presence going deeper and deeper, penetrating the core of my body. It came out of nowhere. I hadn't asked for it, I hadn't expected it, and I didn't manipulate it. But His Spirit completely consumed me.

I had to pull the car off to the side of the road due to the tears that clouded my vision. Peace came upon me like never before—a peace that flowed over my soul. Then I knew it! This fast was of God. There was no reason to doubt. Victory over doubt was at hand. My excitement level grew, anticipating this closeness with God for the remainder of the fast.

In my subsequent research of long-term fasts, I have found that many others who have engaged in such fasts have had similar breakthroughs. They reported feeling as if they were being ushered into the very presence of heaven on earth, just as I did. My quiet times in the morning excelled to greater heights. My total being wanted to strain and nuzzle into the Lord's bosom. My prayer life soared to even greater heights, and the everyday worries of life didn't matter to me anymore. All I wanted was to have a twenty-four-hour quiet time with my Lord and precious Savior. I suspect this is what it will be like in heaven.

It was no longer about me or feeling the cravings of my body crying out for nourishment. What's more, it was no longer about the presidential election. It became all about Jesus and His life-sustaining power. He sent His ministering angels to me, much like He did with the prophet Elijah when He sent the ravens to feed him. Just as He comforted that great prophet, in his time of loneliness and self-doubt, He did the same for me.

Each day the presence of the Lord seemed to grow greater and greater around me. As unbelievable as it may seem, I was a tad chagrined, thinking of going back to eating two to three meals a day. I had come to the point where my body, mind, and spirit were in total submission to the Lord, and I *did not* want the fast to end! I would have never thought this possible had I not walked this road myself.

The Last Lap
Day Thirty-Six—Wednesday, December 13, 2000

Rhonda and I both felt in our spirits that the final days of the election were coming to a close. We both had determined in our hearts that even if the election went beyond the forty days, my fast would end on the fortieth day. We were both at peace with this decision. However, we had never discussed what would happen if the election was called before that time. The election was actually called on day thirty-six. I felt great peace. I was glad the election was over for the sake and morale of the country. That particular election took a great toll on our nation.

Because the election was called on the thirty-sixth day, I would have another four days to go if I wanted to complete a forty-day fast. After prayer, I decided to continue on another four days. I made this decision for two reasons. First, in my heart of hearts, I really didn't want the fast to end. I really didn't. Through God's grace, He had taken me to new depths in my spiritual walk, and I didn't want to lapse back into the old self. Therefore, if I could safely squeeze out another four days, I decided I would do so. The second reason was that I had never been at this stage in fasting in my life, and I never envisioned that I would ever be here again. Hence, I pressed forward.

Two days before my fast was to be completed, Rhonda asked me what I would like to have for my first meal when it was time to end the fast. I told her I had been thinking about that and had decided that I would like to have some mashed potatoes and a slab of meatloaf. I knew I could not gorge myself at the first meal, and although having meatloaf was probably pushing the limits of my stomach capacity, that is what I decided to have. On Sunday, December 17, the fortieth day, the fast came to a close. My family gathered around the kitchen island as they watched me eat and savor each bite. It was good family time, and yes, the meatloaf was awesome.

The Lord Jesus had been good to me. He had taught me so much in those forty days. He had sustained me throughout the fast and brought me into His spiritual presence, which I never would have imagined was possible. This forty-day fast had been the highlight of my spiritual walk. It had not been easy. It had been tough and oftentimes painful. However, the spiritual growth was priceless.

As I look back, I realize that it was the inmates at Stafford Creek Correctional Center who moved me to tears on that historical Election Day. That motivation and encouragement contributed greatly to my responding, "Yes, Lord!" when I heard His still, small voice asking me if I would *stand in the gap* for this country.

As I have already shared, during the prayer time in prison that blessed evening, I heard many of the inmates pray, "If my people, who are called by my name, will humble themselves and pray and seek my face and turn from their wicked ways, then will I hear from heaven and will forgive their sin and will heal their land" (2 Chronicles 7:14).

Men who had lost everything because of their own personal choices, men who had nothing but the power of prayer, and men who believed the Bible in a literal sense had shown the boldness to come before a holy and righteous God and pray 2 Chronicles 7:14 as a cry for their country. God smiled down on those men that evening. While I will never see any of them again until we reach the other side of eternity, the night our lives crossed paths made a lasting impression on me. I thought I was going to minister to them, but in turn, they ended up ministering to me. I would take any one of those men into war with me.

The election of 2000 truly changed my spiritual life when out of simple obedience to that still small voice, I said, "Yes, Lord!"

Some people have asked me if I think that I had any real impact on the election outcome of 2000. I shrug my shoulders and tell them I have not a clue. However, this is what I do know. God spoke to me during my prayer time one day. He asked me if I would *stand in the gap*. I obeyed, not realizing that what I thought would be a fast of three meals would turn into a fast of 120 meals—a forty-day fast. I said, "Yes, Lord." My prayer for those reading this book is that someday God would ask you the same question—will you *stand in the gap* for someone or something?

CHAPTER 4

Honey, Can We Talk?

January 2002

"Honey, can we talk?"

After many years of marriage, I knew these four words meant that my wife had something heavy on her heart that she wanted to share with me. I have learned to be a good listener; I just shut up and don't react (the operative words being "don't react"). Don't say a word until asked. I have learned over the years that our wives don't want us to fix the problem—or more importantly, to fix them. They just want to be heard and for us to listen with a compassionate ear. Being a good listener was never my strong suit in our marriage. I was good at many things, but being a good listener was not one of them. I actually had to work at it. I had to *shut off my brain* and concentrate—fully concentrate. It was a skill that I had to work at and actively work to improve. It wasn't easy, but I tried.

"Pastor is calling the church to do a forty-day fast for clarity and vision. I would like to do the fast," she said.

"Great! Go for it!"

"I was kind of hoping this was something that we could do together."

"Nope, not interested. And besides, honey, he is not calling people in the church to do a forty-day fast. He wants people to pick one day a week and fast on that day each week. That way, every day someone in the church is fasting. He explained that to us."

"I know, but I am feeling led to complete a forty-day fast, like you did. You inspired me with your last fast. I want you to do it with me, together— you and me."

"What? No way! First of all, you have to be called to do a long-term fast. You may be called to do it, but I am NOT! That is a certainty. If you are being called, great! I will support you one hundred percent, but as for me—no cigar. The last fast over the 2000 election was a once-in-a-lifetime situation never to occur again. Do you know how hard it was?"

"Don't you remember the spiritual growth you experienced? That's all you talked about for six months. Will you pray about it?"

"Will I pray about it? Oh, come on! Don't use that on me. Nope, not even feeling an inkling by the Spirit to do another extended fast—much less pray about it. No, no, no! Love you, but no!"

She was doing it again, doing what only Rhonda could do. She was drilling down to the core issue. Maybe it is a skill set, or maybe it is her unassuming way, but she hit a nerve when she said, "Don't you remember the spiritual growth you experienced? That's all you talked about for six months." How could I forget?

Wisdom, insight, and perspective increased exponentially in my daily walk. Purpose increased. The ability to judge the important things of life increased. Pettiness was revealed. But the most important aspect was the hunger to be in the presence of the Lord in a twenty-four-hour quiet time. During that time, I had wondered if that was what it is going to be like when we are in heaven for all eternity, worshipping the Lord with no end, with a hunger for even more. I was having a two-hour quiet time every morning. My prayer life soared. Mountains were blown apart. Fear was arrested. Pride was nailed.

As the first fast slowly ebbed away and life happened, bits and pieces of the spiritual awakening ebbed away as well. Decisions had to be made in the ministry, different priorities crept back in, and the remainder of my spiritual awakening slowly began fading into just a glimmer of light in my memory.

Rhonda brought it all back to life in just a few seconds. The Spirit, through Rhonda, cut me to the quick. The flesh screamed, "No!" The spirit cried, "Yes!" This fundamental conflict of life never goes away—the flesh versus the spirit.

I was at an unexpected and unforeseen crossroads. Almost like the first fast, it just came out of the blue. I didn't go looking for it. It just showed up at my heart's door, unannounced. What was I going to do? In my heart I decided *not* to do the fast.

§

As any hobbyist or weekend warrior who has ever climbed a mountain knows—when you finally come down from the mountain, you mumble something like, "I never want to see another mountain for the rest of my life!" In the mid-eighties, I'd had the opportunity to climb Mt. Adams, located in the Cascade Range of Washington State. It was a great experience. I remember the going up as well as the coming down. It was the highlight of my summer. I had just come to know the Lord and was asked by some friends if I would like to be part of a team of five who would climb the mountain. As a baby believer in Christ, I was so excited to see and experience God's creation up close and personal.

Mt. Adams, if approached from the southern side, does not require any specific mountaineering skills. Don't get me wrong, it is no walk in the park. You do need crampons and an ice axe, but you don't need to be roped together. You also need to be physically, as well as mentally, prepared for a long and grueling hike.

I was told that there are two groups of people who climb Mt. Adams: those that do it in one day, and those who do it in two days. Our group decided that we would fall into the latter category. Our team launched out early one August morning and made it to our camp site, a place that is called the Lunch Counter, at about three in the afternoon. Deciding to call it a day, we smoothed and flattened out the snow for our tents and sleeping bags. I remember later in the evening poking my head out of my tent and seeing God's incredible spectacle of stars that appeared to have just exploded in the sky.

Early on in the planning phase of this trip, I was told that we needed to wake up around three in the morning and be ready to leave the camp by four in order to have a safe climb. This would allow our team a good, safe margin of error to come down the mountain. I was a newbie, and as a newbie, I did what I was told. Three o'clock came around way too soon. We hiked for almost two hours in the dark on snow—the hard, frozen snow. For a newbie, that time hiking up the mountain in the dark was very surreal and very quiet. The only noises I heard were those of the teams that left before us with their ice axes and crampons slicing into the snow above us. It was spectacular to be on the side of the mountain in the crisp morning hours as the sun came up.

We stopped for lunch around eleven that morning, close to being totally spent. We were told that we were about one hundred feet below the False Summit. The False Summit is what I call cruel and unusual punishment for the newbie's psyche. Once you reach the False Summit, you think you are almost to the top, only to find out you have another one- to two-hour hike ahead of you. Our team ultimately made the summit. We then glissaded down in less than a quarter of the time that it took to climb the mountain. It was an experience of a lifetime being on top of a mountain and seeing God's creation in a full, 360-degree, panoramic view.

I crawled to my car and said, "That was awesome. Glad I did it. Never again!"

Two years later, having forgotten about the pain and all the preparation, I was right back in the throes of planning another excursion up Mt. Adams—this time with a whole new set of friends. On this second climb, my team made it to the summit, but I did not. Exhausted from carrying an extra twenty pounds of body weight, I just couldn't do it. I allowed the team to leave without me early that morning, while I stayed back at the Lunch Counter where we had camped. The first trip up Mt. Adams had been a physical challenge. The second trip was a mental one, for I knew what lay ahead, and I chose not to be a part of it. I had mentally psyched myself out.

In the same way, knowing what lay ahead, I was resolved not to do another forty-day fast for the rest of my life.

§

As the days started ticking off the calendar, the church prepared to enter into the season of prayer and fasting. Every Sunday at church, the congregation was reminded of this season of fasting. Each Sunday I was getting a heart nudge from the Holy Spirit, as well as an elbow nudge in my ribs by my wife. With every nudging, I dug my heels in deeper and deeper. However, the Holy Spirit was relentless. During that time I was anxious, not sleeping, and not having good quiet times. The Hound of Heaven had me in His sites and was bearing down on me.

I had experienced the Hound of Heaven two other times in my life: once when I was running from God after the birth of our daughter, Ashley, and once when the Lord was moving me to leave my career as a stockbroker to pursue full-time prison ministry. Both times I resisted tooth and nail. Both times I was a miserable human being, depressed and sleepless. Both times I was in the wilderness by myself, fighting to have my own way, not knowing that God wanted something more and better for my life. The flesh screamed, "No!" The spirit cried, "Yes!"

I either had to support my wife or not. I knew not what I was getting into with the 2000 Election Day fast, but I had clear knowledge regarding this one. In stockbroker language, *caveat emptor*—buyer beware! It was as if I was reliving the Mt. Adams climb all over again. It was all mental. I knew it wasn't going to be easy, but once again, out of obedience to the Lord, I submitted to His will. With that resolve, I took a deep breath, sighed, and shared the news with Rhonda. She was elated; I was not. We started the fast on Sunday, February 17, 2002.

§

As I was mentally preparing for the next journey, the Lord impressed upon me to incorporate journaling, as well as being purposeful in listing out specific prayer requests for the fast—something I had not done in the first fast. Listing out specific prayer request wasn't the problem. Journaling was the problem. Much like fasting, journaling was a new spiritual discipline for me. I had never been mentored on the techniques, let alone the joy of journaling. I had heard of people who journaled every day, but I never had decided to jump into that discipline.

Years before, I'd had a friend and colaborer in the prison ministry, Steve Lamken, who had shared the joys of journaling with me. One evening, after our Wednesday night Bible study at the King County Jail, Steve shared what journaling had meant in his life. I was mildly interested, so I asked Steve out to lunch so I could pick his brain on the topic.

Steve brought with him five of his journals. He told me that he had more at home. I was impressed. I was also shocked and, more importantly, totally overwhelmed. Page after page of Steve's journals filled the leather-bound books. Steve read some of his entries to me. His eyes got wet; my eyes got wet. I walked away from that lunch both amazed and perplexed that an individual would have time to write as much as he had written.

This was a different side of Steve that I had not before seen. Steve was sold out for the Lord, was sold out for his family, and was sold out for the inmates. Steve also had his own siding construction company. To me this seemed truly out of character for the Steve that I knew. I determined in my mind that his type of commitment to journaling was over the top for me. I wasn't ready. However, the seeds sown in me that day took time to germinate, and germinate they did.

Years later, as I prepared to start another extended fast, the Lord impressed on my heart that I was to incorporate journaling into this second one. Journaling was never a discipline that was taught to me from the pulpit, so I would have to learn it on my own as I went.

§

On the first day of the fast, I remember looking at a blank piece of paper in the early morning hours during my quiet time. The day before, I had visited the local Office Max store and picked out a nice leather journal specifically for this fast. I remembered Steve's journals were in nice leather binders, and I wanted the same. The pages were pristine and crinkled with freshness as I turned them. As I stared down at the blank pages, thoughts occurred to me: Now what? What do I write? Where do I begin? What do I say? I was in trouble, I was stymied, and I felt I was in over my head.

The Spirit was faithful and prompted me that instead of praying in my head, I should put the pen to the paper and write out my prayers. Once I learned that simple trait of journaling, my pen took off, as did my journaling. Over the years I have cried my prayers, I have rejoiced and praised the Lord, I have moved mountains, and I have confessed my sin and inadequacies—all with my pen to the paper.

Outside of my tattered Bible, my journals are my second-most prized possessions. If my house was burning down and all my family and pets were out of the house, I would run back in. The first things I would grab would be my Bible and my journals. They are my treasures...my keepsakes. I know exactly where they are, and I would go rescue them. I would risk life and limb to save them. From time to time, I pull them out and read them. It does not take long before the tears begin welling up in my eyes, and my head begins to leak.

Dr. Ronnie Floyd, president of the Southern Baptist Convention, wrote *The Power of Prayer and Fasting*, in which he shares his feelings about the importance of his journals in his life:

> I encourage everyone who fasts and prays—whether it is a one-day, two-day, week-long, or extended fast—to keep a fasting journal. I consider my fasting journals to be pure gold—more valuable than any book in my library besides the Bible. They are filled with the words God has poured into my waiting heart. As I have reread my journals months later, I can see the issue of my human pride is one

area where God continually worked with me. He was relentless. He would not let go. He was the *hound of heaven*. And the more I saw my pride in contrast to His holiness, the more humbled I became in His presence.[1]

CHAPTER 5

§

Greg, Can We Talk?

About Day Seven—Saturday, February 23, 2002

"GREG, CAN WE talk?"

Oh, those words again! But this time they came from my eighty-six-year-old father who lived with us. What's up with that?

"I know this is short notice, but I just got off the phone with Aunt Betty in Florida. Cousin Sharon and her husband are putting together a birthday party for Aunt Betty's eightieth birthday and would like all of us to come down for a visit."

Rhonda, my let's-party-anytime girl, piped up. "Come on, honey, let's go! It will be fun, and who knows the next time we'll able to see the family again."

My wife is truly relational. God built her that way. The more people around, the more fulfilled she is, unlike her husband, who would rather be at home in front of a fireplace. So traveling to Florida for a birthday party did not excite me. Rhonda threw me her signature smile.

Sigh. "When is it, Dad?"

"Three weeks!"

"Three weeks! No way! I can't go on that short of notice. I am so swamped at the ministry. Why didn't they give us more notice? Maybe you could go alone, Dad. You can do it! I will put you on a nonstop flight, so all you'll need to do is just walk off the plane."

"C'mon, Greg! We have frequent flyer miles. It will be an almost-free vacation!" Rhonda chimed in again.

"Three weeks! Three weeks! No way! Are you guys crazy? Plus, there is no such thing as an *almost*-free vacation!"

Dad and Rhonda, Rhonda and Dad—when they gang up on me, I tend to bend, just as a reed bends in the wind.

"Geesh. OK, if we can use the frequent flyer miles, I'm in."

Cheers went up in the room. Dad scurried off to his room to call Aunt Betty with the good news. Rhonda and I were left in the kitchen alone, both relishing the fact that we were going on a spur-of-the-moment vacation. I had never been on a spur-of-the-moment vacation. I am not a spur-of-the-moment type of guy. I don't like being spur-of-the-moment. I like things planned out and in an orderly fashion. I like to think things through so as never to miss a detail. Moments later, I got up from my chair. At that time we were about seven days into the fast, and that day, the pangs of hunger had begun.

"Rhonda, I'm hungry. I'm going to have some juice. What kind of juice do you want?" I stood frozen in my steps as I did some mathematical calculating in about a nanosecond. I turned around to see my wife's eyes as big as saucers and both hands clasped over her mouth. This is a prime example of why I am not a spur-of-the-moment type of guy. I had missed a very important detail—the only detail that mattered. We were committed to a forty-day fast. The spur-of-the-moment vacation was going to fall smack dab in the middle of the fast.

"Quick, tell Dad we can't go! Make something up! Grab him before he makes that call!"

"No, we need to go and be with the family. We will just have to call them and tell them we are fasting and not to make a big deal about it."

"Not make a big deal about it? Are you crazy? This is Aunts Betty's eightieth birthday party. There is going to be food galore at this shin-dig. You want to fast over vacation? Are you out of your mind?" I was incredulous.

"Oh, Lord Jesus, like Thanksgiving, it's happening again," I thought. "Only this time it's with the other side of the family. They are going to think we are stark-raving lunatics!" I knew it was pride rising up in me. I knew I needed to learn to master the act of not caring what other people thought in regard to spiritual things. I prayed, "Lord, forgive me, and please let this fast be a tool with which we can enter into some meaningful conversations with our family about You."

§

The first ten days of the fast were a slugfest for me—a knock-down, drag out, slugfest. Multiple times in my journal, I speak of this fast being harder than the first. On paper I cried out to the Lord for help and sustenance.

During the first ten days, there are many temptations with food. You think about food constantly. The longer you are without, the more you crave. Every TV commercial seems to be about food. You begin to feel as if you will just have to stop watching TV, which wouldn't necessarily be a bad thing. Every billboard you see seems to be about food. Every radio commercial you hear seems to be about food. Every coupon you receive in the mail is a two-for-one special or 20 percent off at your favorite restaurant. You feel that if you are ever to survive the fast, you will need to seek out a monastery. However, you can't do that. You must go on living. Therefore, you learn to pray more that the Spirit will carry you through the temptations of the beginning days.

Headaches, blood sugar swings, and diarrhea are normal daily events. In a long-term fast, if one can motor through to the tenth day, the temptations and the pain do somewhat recede. As the temptation wanes, the spiritual desire starts to increase. It is at this time that the hunger to be intimate with the Lord Jesus intensifies. That desire for intimacy is what propels and sustains one as the days go by.

Heaven Falls

I can't specifically pinpoint the exact day of this second fast, but between day ten and day twenty, things started to *change*. This time it went very slowly, unlike the first fast when the change happened instantaneously. I began to see things with a different perspective. The desire for lengthy quiet times became my first thought of the day. I thought constantly about wanting to be in the presence of the Lord—desiring to be in a pleasing relationship with Him.

As maturing believers, we should always strive to enter into the presence of the Lord, desiring the things that please Him. However, in these breakthroughs, that desire takes root. Heaven fell as it had during the first fast, but there were differences. I saw things in a different way. On this fast, I saw the sin and vileness of mankind—the deep, dark depravity of the human heart. But I also started to see the fruit of the Spirit. One day during this breakthrough I rushed to pick up my Bible to read Galatians 5. I desired to have the fruit of the Spirit in abundance in my life. I began to weep.

Days later, my eyes started to see the colors and the brightness of nature the way I had in the previous fast. On one particular day, I was walking out of the ministry's new offices. We had just been blessed with a rainstorm that had swept through the region. The sun was now bristling through the cloud cover. A small plant caught my eye, and I bent down to see the droplets of rain beading up on the leaves. I soon discovered a spider web, and I watched its owner do what spiders do. I watched for a few minutes and marveled at God's creation. Any other day, I would have noticed neither the plant nor the spider, let alone taken the time to stop. It was a blessing from heaven to stop, rest, and watch God's creation in motion. I thought to myself, "Everything points to a Creator. Why can't mankind see that?"

In those days at the ministry, times were rough. Finances were tough. Four months earlier, 9/11 had shaken our nation to its core. Eighteen months earlier, the dot-com bubble had burst. Life was uncertain; the stock market was uncertain. It is never easy to raise monies for a prison ministry—let alone to do so during times of economic uncertainty. Few people rush to support a ministry that focuses on the darkest of individuals: men and women who have rejected God's standards, who have rebelled against both God and mankind, and who have hurt other people. It is hard to paint a rosy picture and give someone the warm fuzzies about financially supporting a ministry to those who have done great wrongs.

Bills had to be paid; end-of-the-month salaries bore down on me; rent was due. We were stretched. Then one day, heaven fell, and I knew it would all be OK. My soul was at rest. I knew that my Savior, who had moved us into this new office, would provide for our every need, and I waited for that day to arrive. Because I was still new to fasting, I didn't know if the spiritual breakthrough I had experienced in my first fast was the norm or not. I waited expectantly, praying for the breakthrough to come...and it did.

From that day forward, my desire to be in the Lord's presence flew off the charts. Yes, I had heavy responsibilities at the ministry—the *business* of life was front and center. I prayed more fervently than ever before that the salaries of my people would be paid; they were. Provisions were sent from God on high. The greater the need, the more I prayed, and greater were the victories—expectant prayer being answered in miraculous ways. Heaven fell.

The Egg Salad Sandwich
Day Twenty-Six—Thursday, March 14, 2002

It was D-Day. Rhonda, Dad, and I boarded a plane to go visit the family in Florida for my Aunt Betty's eightieth birthday party. We were excited to steal away, but there was also some fear and trepidation for Rhonda and me, knowing that we were still fasting. Back in 2002, the airlines were feeding their passengers fairly good food; however, we abstained. As we stepped out into the Florida sunshine, it felt good just having the warmth beating down on our faces and warming our innards.

The following day we decided to go shopping at one of my cousin Sharon's favorite outdoor shopping areas. Since we were from the Northwest, we were not accustomed to the heat, and especially the humidity, in Florida. I love to shop with my wife, but most of the time I am four aisles ahead of her. That day, I was three stores ahead of her. As I was perusing the shop, I heard a commotion behind me. I turned and saw two of my cousins, Paula and Christy, rapidly approaching me with wide eyes. They explained to me that Rhonda had just fainted in one of the stores. They assumed it was because of the heat and humidity.

By the time I got to her, she was sitting up with a pop in one hand and an egg salad sandwich in the other. The fast was over for her, but I was so proud of her. She had lasted twenty-seven days. I am totally confident that, had she not been in the humid climate of Florida, she would have completed the forty-day fast. Lesson learned in fasting: when the body gives out, it is time to end the fast.

Day Twenty-Nine—Sunday, March 17, 2002

The big day arrived for Aunt Betty's big birthday. *Déjà vu!* It was Thanksgiving all over again. I couldn't believe I was in the same situation. There I was sitting at a fine restaurant, white linen tablecloths making an elegant backdrop for the crystal glasses stuffed with linen napkins. The restaurant had an unbelievable menu and was known for its fish and steak. I ordered a glass of cranberry juice. The waiter didn't understand and asked me repeatedly if I would like a side salad or a cup of bisque. He truly didn't understand. I finally had to lean back and whisper to him that I was fasting. With a strange and awkward look on his face, he moved on.

Some have called me rigid when it comes to making and keeping commitments. Rhonda may have had to end her fast because of medical reasons, but that did not give me the luxury of doing the same. Fasting is between the believer and the Lord, and I felt I needed to be fully committed to what I had agreed upon with the Him. So there I sat with my glass of juice while everybody else chowed down on their steaks and seafood. I looked over at my sweet wife. She gave me her signature smile that says in the end, it will all be OK. When Rhonda smiles, it is radiant and illuminates the entire room. All was well with my soul.

We arrived back in Seattle as the final days of the fast wound down. When I started this fast, I had never looked to see when day forty would fall. About day thirty, I started poking around the calendar to see the exact date the fast would end. It just so happened that day forty would be the evening of Maundy Thursday—the day before Good Friday. In years past I had taken Good Friday off from the ministry and headed over to a retreat center for a day of prayer and—guess what—a day of fasting.

I had a decision to make: Do I end the fast on the scheduled evening of Thursday, March 28, or do I press on for one more day through Good Friday? I decided this would be an extra-special Good Friday as I reflected not only on the past forty days but also on the suffering of the Lord Jesus on the day two thousand years earlier when He had gone to the cross for the sins of all mankind.

Last Day—Friday, March 29, 2002

I took Good Friday off from the ministry and went to a retreat center on top of the Issaquah plateau. I reflected on the happenings of the last forty days. I was quiet before the Lord and felt humbled beyond the core of my being. I spent all day in solitude and quietness at the retreat center. I sat and read my Bible, I paced the room, I lay on the bed, and I offered silent prayers of gratitude for His all-sufficiency. I reread my journal notes and wept. I thanked Him for this fast and what He had taught me.

In the very beginning of the fast, the Lord had prompted me to be in specific prayer for certain things, as well as to journal. That day, I looked back on the six specific prayer requests that I had listed out on day one of the fast. The prayers were not crisis prayers, but they were very important to Rhonda and me. Some were life-changing decisions Rhonda and I were making together. I prayed day after day over each of those six prayers. I needed God's direction on each one of them. Periodically, as the years flowed by, I would review that list. As of this writing, five of the six prayer requests have been answered.

Unlike the end of the first fast, when I said, "Never again," I felt a new joy in my heart and soul as I couldn't wait until the next time when the Lord Jesus would call me to another extended fast. He brought me from "Never again" to "When, Lord?"

I closed out my fast with the signature mashed-potatoes-and-meatloaf meal, having only a couple of bites of each. My family surrounded me again, and all was well with my soul.

CHAPTER 6

The Nudge

IN THE YEAR 2000, I received a phone call from Pastor Keith Bachelor, the mission's pastor at Canyon Hills Community Church. Keith and the mission team had been establishing a relationship with a Russian pastor who had come to the United States at the request of the church's mission's council. Keith called me the day before Pastor Yuri was leaving town. In his closing comments to Pastor Keith, Pastor Yuri said that, in addition to reaching the Russian people for the cause of Christ, he also had a burden and a broken heart to reach Russian inmates with the Gospel.

After hearing that, Pastor Keith made his call to me. Keith ultimately sold me on the idea that I needed to drop everything and speak with this Russian pastor *that day*! I was very hesitant as I have had many of those you-need-to-drop-everything types of phone calls in the past, only to come to nothing. However, because it was my friend Pastor Keith doing the asking this time, I agreed.

I instructed my staff to clear my schedule for the next hour. Pastor Yuri and his interpreter, Inna, came to the Prisoners For Christ offices. Pastor Yuri and I spoke about prison ministry in Russia—not for an hour, but for more than three hours that day. Pastor Yuri poured out his heart with his desire to reach the Russian inmates for the cause of Christ. Pastor Yuri said he had been praying before he came to America that he would find someone here who had "built the bicycle"—meaning someone who had already built a system for reaching inmates.

"We have built the bike, and we freely give it to you," I said to Pastor Yuri.

My mind quickly shifted gears, wondering how I was going to fulfill that promise—how was I going to build a Russian bike. My mind then raced to thoughts about the costs of translating all our materials into Russian in order to fulfill Pastor Yuri's vision.

Without warning, Pastor Yuri blurted out, "Pastor Greg, I formally want to invite you to come to my motherland, Russia, to train up our church leaders in how to do prison ministry."

"No, no, Pastor Yuri. I was thinking more along the lines of gathering some material for you to train your volunteers." After a long and uncomfortable pause, Pastor Yuri said, "Pastor Greg, you must come to Russia. I plead with you to come and help us with prison ministry."

Everything inside of me was screaming, "There is no way I am going to the gulags of Russia!" Again, the flesh was screaming, "No!" while the Spirit was crying, "Yes!" I was scared out of my mind when I went to visit a jail for the first time in the mid-1980s here in America. I was even more terrified at the mere thought of going to Russia and a Russian prison.

Before I could react a second time to say no, the Lord quickly took me to the Macedonia call in the book of Acts, where Paul saw a man in a dream who cried out, "Come help us." The Bible says Paul immediately got ready to go the next day. How could I say no, but how could I say yes? I asked Pastor Yuri when he thought would be a good time to come to Russia, hoping he would propose a time in the distant future—like maybe in the next five years. However, he said, "Next year. You come in June of next year, Pastor Greg."

Little did I know that the conversation with Pastor Yuri would be the start of PFC going to the four corners of the world to share the prison training with which the Lord had so blessed us. Over the ensuing months, I attempted to learn as much as I could about the culture of Russia and how to lead a team to a foreign land. The following year, I led a team of nine Americans safely to Russia and back without incident. It was those beginning years of the international work of PFC that the Lord used to open my eyes to the vast need for quality prison ministry training for our brothers and sisters in foreign countries. We ultimately went back to Russia in 2002, 2003, 2004, and 2005.

In 2003 a couple we knew, Greg and Jean Ishmael, invited my wife to be part of a team going to an orphanage in Kenya run by Christian Ministries in Africa. After many weeks of haggling over whether she should go or not, the four of us were in a meeting when Rhonda said, "OK, OK, OK! I will go...if he goes," she said as she pointed to me.

I thought to myself, "There she goes again, dragging me into something I don't want to be a part of." I had absolutely no interest in going to Africa.

The three of them looked at me as if to say, "Well?"

"What? I have no interest in going to Africa; there is enough to keep the ministry busy in Russia." A long, awkward silence followed. Finally, the only thing I could think to say was, "OK, I will only go if I can gain entrance to some of the prisons." I had, in my infinite wisdom, already surmised that there were no prisons in Africa, and even if there were one or two, they would be so remote they wouldn't be able to obtain permission for me. I was safe, so I thought.

Less than four days from when I had opened my mouth, the word came back that the answer was yes. Their contacts in Africa would be able to obtain permission for me to enter some of the prisons. So, off to Africa we went.

Africa sealed the deal. I finally realized that every country on the face of the earth had prisons. If there are prisons, then there are men, there are women, and there are children who desperately need to hear the Gospel of Jesus Christ. I also realized that the state of prison ministry in developing countries was similar to the state of prison ministry forty years earlier here in America, when it was in its embryonic stage. For whatever reason, God was positioning PFC to be an instrument of exhortation and encouragement to our brothers and sisters in other countries who were laboring all alone, doing prison ministry under extreme conditions.

In 2003, PFC took one trip to Russia. In 2004 we increased our capacity by hundred percent to two trips—one to Russia and one to Kenya.

Much to my surprise, in 2005, the Lord allowed PFC to once again double its reach by hundred percent, taking four trips that year to Russia, Kenya, India, and the Philippines.

§

Unlike the previous two fasts that had come to me out of left field, the third fast was a slow burn. I had already seen the incredible blessings of the Lord's hand on the believers in Russia and Kenya. I knew 2005 would bring an equal amount of blessings by going back to those two countries, as well as adding trips to India and the Philippines. My heart's desire was to reach inmates for the cause of Christ. However, just as important to me was the challenge of taking American Christians out of their comfort zones in order for them to experience all that God was doing around the globe. It was going to be an exciting year. I was nervous, and I was anxious.

Was I pushing the envelope by taking four trips in one year? How was I going to raise enough funds to sustain the ministry as well as to fund four additional trips this year? There was a great deal of discussion at our board meetings on this very subject. The Lord had given the board a spirit of unity and peace over these matters; however, their leader was still anxious as we had never before been in these waters. I needed a miracle. I needed to see the hand of God.

The urge to fast was a slow burn that built in momentum. It started in September of 2004 and increased in force and desire each month until I knew in my spirit that it was the right thing to do. Unlike the first two fasts, which I had not looked forward to, I was quite excited for this one. I was excited for the intimacy with the Lord. I was excited for the hunger for His word. I was excited for "heaven falling."

As the weeks and months of 2004 slowly ticked away, I pondered the right timing for my fast. I knew I wanted to bypass the holidays—Thanksgiving, Christmas, and New Year's. By this time, I was becoming a student of the miracles and blessings of fasting. I started doing research on the Internet. I came across a number of sites that espoused the beginning of the year as a time to begin a fast for an extended period. By mid-December of 2004, I was in a full-court press, praying and preparing my heart for the fast to come. In regard to the previous extended fasts, I'd never had time to pray in advance. This time I did, and it was refreshing.

The Beginnings
Day One—Monday, January 3, 2005

I was excited. I had been nudged by the Holy Spirit to complete another extended fast. This time there was no resistance on my part. I received the prompting with joy in my heart. The holidays were past. The new year was starting. Everything was fresh, and the ministry had four trips planned for 2005. It looked as if it was going to be a very good year. I was ready. However, I was also concerned.

I was out on a limb. I had been there with the Lord many times before, and He had always come through in the eleventh hour. But with four trips this year, training team members to go on their first cross-cultural trip, raising funds for those trips, and raising support for the overall ministry, it all seemed over the top.

In addition to the demands of the ministry, I had an additional burden. Several years before, I had been flipping through the channels late at night and came across an advertisement stating that the Duvall City Council had an open city council position. Being a dyed-in-the-wool Republican and patriot, I had always been semi-interested in politics, and I often wondered, What if? I felt a need to serve our community, which was the bedroom community of Redmond, Washington, home of Microsoft. After some discussion with my wife, we decided together that I should throw my hat in the ring and fill out an application, thinking, Why not? It can't be too much of a time commitment.

I had phone interviews with all the council members, as well as the mayor. I made no bones about the fact that I was a born-again, Bible-believing

Christian. Much to my surprise, I was voted in to fill the vacant spot. Being on the city council was a joy for the most part. I learned a lot about dealing with prickly people. There was a cost to that learning, however, with two city council meetings a month, in addition to two committee meetings a month, countless phone calls from the mayor and city staff, and phone calls from the community—life was full.

Overseeing Prisoners For Christ and being on the Duvall City Council was very doable. Overseeing Prisoners For Christ, being on the Duvall City Council, *and* rapidly expanding the international side of the ministry was *not* doable! I needed a fresh wind, a mighty move of God in my life. I was hoping for another breakthrough like I had experienced in the past. In other words, I needed a good deal of prayer in this season of my life. I had bitten off more than I could chew.

With the second fast, I had learned the power of journaling. Since that fast, I had carried on with the new discipline in my quiet times. I was excited to go even deeper with the Lord. Elmer Towns, cofounder of Liberty University, speaks of the power of journaling in his book *Fasting for Spiritual Breakthroughs*:

Throughout history, great Christian leaders have kept personal journals to record observations about their Christian lives and ministries. These leaders used their journals to record God-given insights and expressions of their personal struggles. Their journals were rarely meant to be published; however, they have helped many Christians today work through similar struggles. The journals of David Brainerd, John Wesley, and others are inspiring records of personal experiences with God that help people today in their own unique experiences with Him.[2]

The benefits of journaling are numerous. First, journaling helps to slow down and refocus fast-paced people. Second, it gives people opportunities to get in touch with and record their feelings. Third, it provides a means of recording important lessons God is daily teaching. Over time, journals may record the significant growth in people's lives that might otherwise go unnoticed and/ or unmeasured. Also, journals provide records of God's answers to prayers and other good gifts received from the Father.[3]

In the second fast, the Lord taught me to approach it with purpose. This third one would be no different. I wrote out eight specific prayer requests, with number one being for my aging father.

Dad had come from a different era. He had served in World War II and come through the Great Depression. He was also a very devout (but nonpracticing) Catholic. He was a sweet man. Even to this day, when people talk about my dad, they talk about how sweet he was. And at the time of my fast, my burden for him to accept Jesus was exploding in my heart. Mom, who had died in 1999, had also come from that era. Shortly after starting the ministry in 1990, I recruited Mom to come out of retirement and be the PFC's secretary. At that time, she didn't know the Lord either; she, too, was steeped in Catholicism. However, before her death, she came to know Jesus and was baptized.

My dad was a different story. Witnessing to him was hard. Whenever Rhonda and I attempted to share Christ with him, he always had a knack for squirming out of the conversation. Something was holding him back, but we didn't know what. I knew we wouldn't have him long, as he was advancing in years. Dad was my number one prayer request—my prayer priority. My prayer was that the Lord would not take him before he had an opportunity to profess Jesus.

Another prayer request was for the four PFC international trips. I was a novice in leading teams, and I was a novice in foreign travels. This was truly a do-it-yourself project. My teams and I were learning together and learning by our mistakes. I knew 2005 was going to be a financially tough year overall for the ministry, but adding another layer of financial commitment was weighing on my shoulders. I believed the Lord was leading us in these endeavors; however, it didn't relieve the stress of taking on more financial commitments. I took a deep breath, and we forged ahead with the power of the Holy Spirit in front of us as our shield, and behind us as our rear guard. When I think back on the early years of the international development, I have fond memories of the childlike faith that Jesus encourages.

In 2000, there was a small little book that was published by Bruce Wilkinson, which had a dramatic impact on my life: *The Prayer of Jabez*. I started praying a simple prayer: "Lord, increase our territories." There are 196 countries on the face of the earth, and all 196 countries have an issue with sin. Wherever there is an issue with sin, there is a reason for prisons.

I have no idea how the Lord plans to use Prisoners For Christ in reaching the prisons of the world. But back in 2005, as I was listing prayer requests for the third extended fast, I listed seven countries that I asked the Lord to open up for us. We are currently in five of those original seven countries. Throughout my third of four fasts, I fervently prayed for the Lord to expand our territories. He is doing that even now, eleven years after this fast took place.

The first two extended fasts seemingly came out of nowhere. But the third fast was a prompting from the Holy Spirit. Before this fast, I had time to pray and time to prepare, both physically and mentally. By the time the fast started, I was excited. I was mentally prepared. I eagerly waited for the fast to begin. Was I expecting this fast to be easier than the first two fasts? No. Actually, in my journal I wrote that this fast was more difficult than the previous two.

CHAPTER 7

§

Heaven Delayed

THE HOURS, DAYS, and weeks clicked by. The third fast was even harder than the first in terms of willpower and the temptations that the enemy threw at me. I remember several instances when I was placed in situations with incredible food in front of me. I was tempted by the enemy to just go ahead and eat, to end the fast and restart the next day. I fought those temptations. The battle was fierce, but I knew in my heart of hearts that the harder the battle, the more there was at stake. By His power, I succeeded in overcoming those early attempts by the enemy.

Then a spiritual trial of self-doubt came from out of nowhere, totally unexpected. I was anxiously waiting the rending of the curtains of heaven, in expectation of heaven falling. This spiritual experience from the prior fasts was what was propelling me to go deeper in this fast. However, as the days went by, heaven didn't fall. I was perplexed. Had I done something wrong (as if to say fasting was a spiritual formula)? Had I not heard from the Holy Spirit to undertake this fast? The enemy was wrapping me around the axle with his questions, fueling my self-doubt. I wondered if the same spiritual breakthroughs that I had experienced in the previous fasts might not occur on this fast. This perplexed me even more. Day twenty came and went; days twenty-three and twenty-four flew by without heaven falling.

There was an internal struggle going on as I asked myself if I was fasting for the wrong reason—for the spiritual experience. It was revealed to me by the Holy Spirit that seeking a spiritual experience in fasting would have been sin caused by pride. I wanted nothing to do with pride. I'd had too much pride in the past chapters of my life, and I knew exactly where pride would lead me. I immediately fell prostrate and asked the Lord to take this away. I cried out to Him to forgive me of any wrong motives for this fast and confessed to the Lord the sin of pride. Once this realization and confession took place, I was freed.

My quiet times once again soared to new heights as the intimacy I craved with the Lord was restored. When I am not fasting, my desire to spend time with the Lord is at its normal level. However, in these seasons of extended fasting, that desire turns into cravings. I didn't want my quiet times to end. On extended fasts, it is not uncommon to have a two-hour quiet time and still want more. I truly believe this strong desire to be with the Lord is just a small sampling of what heaven will be like.

In fasting, as heaven falls, clarity comes, as does perspective. Wisdom is heightened as pride is nailed to the cross. Self decreases, and He increases. The Word of God is devoured. Holy boldness is at its all-time high. Physical eyes are replaced with spiritual eyes. Peace that surpasses all understanding is at your heart's door. Prayers are lifted high. You have peace about your prayers, regardless of the outcomes, your situation, or your trials. That is truly one of the many blessings of fasting.

You finally arrive at the point where, even as hard as the fast might be, you don't want it to end. That is another of the many blessings of obeying the Lord in fasting.

Bill Bright, the late founder and CEO of Campus Crusade for Christ, recounts many testimonies from different people in his book *The Transforming Power of Fasting and Prayer*. This particular testimony is from one such gentlemen, Michael:

> The Lord was so gracious to reveal Himself to me during my devotions. I was overwhelmed by Him! Never before have I been so consistently aware of His presence. I gained a new understanding of His awesome holiness and His unrelenting desire for me to be holy. Never before have I been so conscious of my own sinfulness and self-centeredness. I would spend hours with Him sometimes.

Often I found myself weeping with emotions I'd never known. Never before have I had such a deep burden for the need of God's people to repent.[4]

Answered Prayer

My prayer priority for the third fast was my dad's spiritual condition—that he would receive Jesus as Lord and Savior of his soul. Nothing happened immediately—in fact, several years passed. The burden for my dad grew each day. He was aging. I knew time was short, but I continued to pray that the Lord would not take him yet.

Finally, one day over dinner, Rhonda saw the anxiety on my face and how troubled I was over him—to the point of agonizing over it. She suggested that I needed to go to Dad's house—he was living on his own at this time—and, eyeball-to-eyeball, share one more time with him. She said, "You've prayed, we've prayed, you've fasted—one last time, go share with him. Then know in your heart of hearts you have done all that is humanly possible."

Dad always liked to cook dinner for Rhonda and me. So one day, I invited myself over for dinner. After we ate, I sat him down on his favorite couch, and eyeball-to-eyeball, with passion in my belly, I shared the Gospel one last time with him. In closing I said, "Dad, the only way to get to heaven is through faith in Jesus Christ. Would you like to receive Jesus in your heart and trust in him for your eternal destiny?" There was a pause that seemed like eternity to me, and then he said, "Yes!"

At the age of ninety-one, my sweet dad became a believer in Christ. We had Dad with us for another three years before the Lord took him home at the age of ninety-four. In the weeks that followed his conversion experience, I went out and bought him his own personal Bible, which he always kept on the coffee table. He even started coming to church with Rhonda and me.

In addition to my dire prayer request for my dad, the other prayer priority during my third fast was the question of what was I going to do with the commitment I had made to the city council, and should I even seek out any further potential in the political arena? After the fast, Rhonda and I made a big decision not to pursue any further steps in the political process. It wasn't even a hard decision. I fasted for clarity of mind and wisdom over this decision, and the Lord offered that to me.

Shortly thereafter, I felt the Lord leading me to resign from the Duvall City Council. Although I had enjoyed that season of my life immensely, I felt the Lord leading me to devote more attention to expanding the ministry of PFC across the world. The prayer of Jabez, "Oh Lord, increase my territory," took hold. I fasted for Dad, and He granted that request. I fasted for clarity, wisdom, and peace. He granted those to me as well.

The Hows and Whys of Fasting

There's power when a leader calls for a corporate fast. It's like a nation or church declaring war. I believe God magnifies their efforts more than we can possibly imagine.[5]

Dave Williams

CHAPTER 8

What Does the Bible Say about Fasting?

So, WHY DID God create our bodies to need food? Have you ever thought about that question? I don't know about you, but I love food—not always with my best health in mind. I love a big, fat, juicy burger or a prime rib steak. As I write this, my dear wife is prepping for an early Thanksgiving meal with all of the fixings. I can smell the food as the different scents waft upstairs to my writing den.

However, there are two food items on the traditional Thanksgiving menu that I am not a fan of—pumpkin pie and candied yams. I don't like yams on their own, much less yams with marshmallows on top. (Who on earth ever thought to put marshmallows on yams?) However, I have friends and family who love this dish. Don't we have an incredibly creative God? He created the entire universe and everything in it, including the incredible miracle of the human body. He created us with a variety of tastes. Being all-powerful, He certainly could have created our bodies not to need food, but He didn't.

So why did God create our bodies to need food? I believe there are five reasons that answer this question.

1. *Everything points to a loving Creator.* Our bodies are meticulously and intricately made. All the different parts work in unison with one another as one system. I have often marveled that there

are any atheists in the medical profession. I have never been able to reconcile how a doctor, who knows firsthand the precision with which the body functions, could not believe that it was created by a loving God. From the miracle of the eyeball to the complexity of the brain, the lungs that take in oxygen needed for the organs to remain alive, the individualized taste buds, the digestive tract that acts like a factory extricating the nutrients the body needs to function, and the simple fingernail—it is all compelling evidence that points to a personal Creator. I haven't even touched on the facts about the unique, personalized DNA, or the reproductive abilities that produce offspring. It takes more faith to believe that we developed out of a pool of algae than it does to believe in a loving, Creator God.

Because God desires no one to be lost, He filled His creation with signs everywhere that point to Him. One of those signs is the human body. The body is so intricately designed, so finely tuned, that no one has any excuse not to believe in a Creator. It doesn't take a highly educated medical doctor to understand that the human body is a miracle that points to a Creator.

2. *The diversity of food.* Rhonda and I once visited a new grocery store that was known for its volume of merchandise, as well as the variety of organic products that it carried. We walked up and down each aisle, marveling at the assortment of foods. I will never forget rounding the corner of one aisle and seeing row after row of bulk nuts. Almost every kind of nut imaginable could be bought at this store. I was astounded. The array of different nuts started me thinking about the creative power of our God and how He developed the earth to produce an incredible variety of foods.

As we strode down the produce aisle, we were stunned by how many kinds of potatoes there were. The same was true of the apples. Once again, I was struck by the creativity of our Lord and all the food He made to match our individualized taste buds. We continued on through the fresh fish and meat section, where the same overwhelming variety was on display. Everything points to a Creator, even the diversity of food!

3. *For our pleasure.* I love olives. My wife hates olives. My wife loves beets. I hate beets. I love salmon, but when friends who dislike fish come for dinner, I grill something else. I really dislike liver and onions, but in the South you will find it on the menus of many restaurants, indicating that many people must enjoy it. Rhonda bakes an incredible chocolate pecan pie, and Sandy, one of our in-laws, makes an incredible Thai chicken wrap with peanut sauce. Whenever I have a chance, I request those dishes for family gatherings. Grandpa Chuck fixes gnocchi, another favorite of the extended family.

   Oftentimes I can't wait till I can eat at an authentic Italian restaurant, where I can order a Caesar salad with a side of anchovies. I love those salty little fish. Others despise them and think I have a few screws loose in my head for liking them. I order dishes with up to five-plus stars at Thai restaurants, while Rhonda orders a less spicy minus-one star.

   We are His children, each with differing tastes in food. He individualized each one of our taste buds and gave us the gift of food for our enjoyment. He wants us to delight in the foods He created for us. Everything points to a Creator, even the diversity of our taste buds!

4. *For our fellowship.* In about four hours, our extended family is going to descend on our house and gather for an early Thanksgiving meal. We are not cooking the traditional turkey; instead, we are serving a succulent prime rib. We will offer thanks before the meal and promptly sit down to dig in. The room will be quiet for a time while everyone is busy stuffing their faces. Then slowly, the conversation will start to build and grow into a happy mixture of talk and laughter. Some of my fondest memories from my

childhood were when our family would travel from Peoria, Illinois, to Indianapolis, Indiana, to spend time with my aunt, uncles, and cousins. I remember those days as if they were yesterday—stories and memories surrounded the dinner table.

I believe God intended for the family to gather around the dinner table to strengthen their bonds, to have fun, and to have a time for teaching and discussion. The family meal should be the centerpiece of the day—a place for children and parents to share their stories of the day. How unfortunate for the American family that we have lost the passion for the family meal. Our lives have been taken over by packed schedules, to-do lists, appointments, and extracurricular school activities. We have little margin to just sit and enjoy being with one another without the TV blaring or the cell phone ringing and pinging. We are rich in material possessions but poverty-stricken in family relations.

The Bible says in Deuteronomy 12:7: "There, in the presence of the Lord your God, you and your families shall eat and shall rejoice in everything you have put your hand to, because the Lord your God has blessed you." What a glorious promise! God's Word is ever so true. Let us reclaim the years the locusts have stolen by restoring the joys of family bonding at mealtime.

In my position as president of Prisoners For Christ, I spend many hours around the lunch table with our friends and colaborers in the ministry. Countless friendships have started and developed over a meal. Many of my friends and I often go out to lunch to talk about our families, interests, and hobbies. We hold one another accountable. We connect. There is nothing like chowing down on one of my favorite sandwiches, the Reuben, as we dig deeper into one another's lives. Many a tear has been shed over deep conversations of the soul, which might not have occurred had we not met for a meal. Being able to eat and enjoy food is truly a gift from God. He has created food so that we can be in unique fellowship with one another. Our desire for this kind of fellowship points to a relational Creator.

5. *For worship.* Every bite of food is certainly an occasion for the children of God to give thanks to the Creator. In our household, we always offer a moment of prayer to thank the Lord for His daily provision. In Timothy 4:3–4 the Apostle Paul writes, "They forbid people to marry and order them to abstain from certain foods, which God created to be received *with thanksgiving by those who believe* and who know the truth. For everything God created is good, and nothing is to be rejected if it is received with thanksgiving, because it is *consecrated by the Word of God* and prayer" (emphasis added).

The first morsel of food that enters our mouths at each meal should be a reminder to give the Lord a verbal thank offering for His great and awesome sustenance. Every meal is the opportunity to do just that. Godward gratitude should come as easily as swallowing our food—but it doesn't. Let us be reminded at each meal to give the Lord Almighty a heartfelt thank you for the food He has provided for us.

Is Fasting Ever Commanded in the Bible?

John MacArthur, in his sermon on biblical fasting, states, "Fasting is the total abstinence from food, that's the idea. In fact, the Greek word, it's a very simple word *nestea*, from *nea* which means not and *estea*, which means to eat. It means not to eat; to abstain from food."[6] If enjoying our eating is truly a gift from God, then why would we want to abstain from eating? Although this book is primarily targeted on one purpose of fasting (to stave off disaster), there are over twenty-one different reasons for fasting listed in the Bible.

However, from Genesis to Revelation there is only one time that God commanded a fast as an ongoing ordinance from one generation to the next; it is the Feast of the Day of Atonement, Yom Kippur. The

Day of Atonement is explained in Leviticus chapters 16 and 23. This is a most holy day, as prescribed by God, in which His chosen people were to do no work and to deny themselves. This was the day once a year in which atonement was made for the entire nation of Israel for their sins of the past year. It was also a lasting ordinance for generation to generation. The fast had to occur from the evening of the ninth day to the evening of the tenth day of the seventh month Tishri, from sunset to sunset.

The fast in Leviticus 16 is linked to a sorrowful, mournful spirit of confessing one's sin. However, Jesus Christ's sacrifice on the cross has replaced this kind of atonement. As New Testament Christians, we are no longer required to keep this holy day as laid out in the Old Testament. Throughout the entire Bible, there are no further scriptures that command fasting at a specific time or place. However, there are numerous occasions in the Bible where fasting is demonstrated as a tool wielded by many men and women of faith during great spiritual and personal trials.

Fasting today is as popular as liver and onions, or maybe as popular as going into prison. To some it may also be seen as barbaric. Fasting is not on many radar screens. It is looked upon as a dinosaur that went extinct long ago. However, I stand before you today to shout it from the mountaintops: "Fasting should not be overlooked in the believer's arsenal of spiritual weaponry!"

The American church today has become disconnected from the discipline of fasting. This disconnect does not exist in the Christian churches of the developing world. For Americans, fasting is a completely foreign concept. It is rarely preached, and it is hardly ever taught in discipleship materials as a spiritual discipline for a new believer. As Americans, we have great material prosperity, but our prayer lives and our faith walks are often poverty-stricken. Conversely, our Christian brothers and sisters on the other side of the world in developing countries are very poor in material possessions, but they are *millionaires* in their prayer lives and their faith walks. Our American prosperity has come between us and our God. It has become an idol for many.

Whenever I begin a discussion on fasting with someone, I see that person start to squirm. A conversation on fasting is often threatening for many believers. Fasting has been out of practice in the American church for many years and has been relegated to the back of the bus of spiritual disciplines for quite some time.

Types and Styles of Fasting

Fasting, by definition, is the refraining from all food. There are basically three different *types* of fasts and four different *styles* of fasting modeled in the Bible.

THREE DIFFERENT *TYPES* OF FASTS

1. **Regular fast.** A regular fast is the refraining from all solid food. Many of the fasts listed in the Bible are examples of this kind of fast. However, when fasting today, many people drink juice.

2. **Partial fast.** A partial fast is one that is found in Daniel chapter 10, otherwise known as the "Daniel Fast." In verse 3, Daniel says, "I ate no choice food; no meat or wine touched my lips." In other words, Daniel eliminated certain food *types* from his diet. This type of fast will be discussed further in chapter 13.

3. **Full fast.** This is a fast, also known as the "Absolute Fast," where one abstains from all food and drink. This particular fast should never be undertaken for any length of time. There are a number of examples in the Bible where a full fast was undertaken. Moses fasted for forty days (some say eighty days consecutively) without any food or water. This was a divine fast that was only sustained through the power of God (Deuteronomy 9:9, 18). Esther instructed Mordecai in Esther 4:16 as follows: "Go, gather together all the Jews who are

in Susa, and fast for me. Do not eat or drink for three days, night or day. I and my maids will fast as you do. When this is done, I will go to the king, even though it is against the law. And if I perish, I perish." The Apostle Paul, who was blinded after meeting Jesus face-to-face on the road to Damascus, did not eat or drink anything for three days after that encounter (Acts 9:9).

In addition to the three different *types* of fasts, there are four different *styles* of fasts.

Four Different *Styles* of Fasts

1. ***The individual fast.*** This is the fast for the individual believer who has a concern or problem, or desires to obtain a deeper intimacy with the Lord. This is a highly personal and private fast between the individual and the Lord (Nehemiah 1:4).

2. ***The partnership fast.*** This fast is demonstrated by the fast called for by Queen Esther between her and her cousin Mordecai. They were facing a life-and-death struggle. Many Jews were about to lose their lives, and something had to be done. Mordecai told Queen Esther that she needed to make an appeal to King Xerxes. In her reply back to Mordecai, she says, "Go gather together all the Jews who are in Susa and fast for me. Do not eat or drink for three days, night or day. I and my maids will fast as you do" (Esther 4:16).

3. ***The corporate fast.*** An example of a corporate fast is when the king of Nineveh, after hearing Jonah's eight-word message—"Forty more days and Nineveh will be overturned"—issued this decree. "Do not let any man or beast, herd or flock, taste anything; do not let them eat or drink. But let man and beast be covered with sackcloth. Let everyone call urgently on God" (Jonah 3:7–8).

    Another example of a biblical, corporate fast was when an invading army was about to attack Judah. "Alarmed Jehoshaphat resolved to inquire of the Lord, and he proclaimed a fast for all Judah" (2 Chronicles 20:3).

4. *The "standing in the gap" fast.* This fast is referenced when Jesus spoke to His disciples after they were not able to expel a demon from a young boy. Jesus said, "This kind can come out by nothing but prayer and fasting" (Mark 9:29, NKJV). In essence, Jesus was saying that certain demonic strongholds can only be overcome by prayer and fasting. The question that needs to be asked is, can a demon-possessed person fast for deliverance for himself? The answer is, obviously, no! Therefore, someone must *stand in the gap* for that demon-possessed person to fast and pray for his or her complete healing.

Another example of a *standing in the gap* fast is found in 2 Samuel 12:15–17 when David was fasting for his dying son:

> After Nathan had gone home, the Lord struck the child that Uriah's wife had borne to David, and he became ill. David pleaded with God for the child. He *fasted* and went into his house and spent the nights lying on the ground. The elders of his household stood beside him to get him up from the ground, but he refused, and he would not eat any food with them. (Emphasis added.)

Could his son fast for himself? No. Therefore, David took it upon himself to fast for his ailing son.

Who Are People in the Bible Who Fasted?

There are many people in the Bible who fasted. Some were positive examples of fasting, and others fasted with the wrong motives. Below is a list of those people who fasted, the length of time of their fasts, and their purposes for fasting.

POSITIVE EXAMPLES OF FASTING

Reference	Who	Purpose
Exodus 34:27–28	Moses (forty days)	In service during kingdom work
Judges 20:18–28	The nation of Israel (one day)	Intervention, staving off disaster, and wisdom in what to do
1 Samuel 1:6–18	Hannah (ongoing fast)	Intervention, private afflictions, and to bear children
1 Samuel 7:2–6	The nation of Israel (one day)	Confession of sin
1 Samuel 31:13	Men of Jabesh Gilead (seven days)	Mourning over a death
2 Samuel 1:12	David and his men (one day)	Mourning over a death
2 Samuel 3:30–35	David	Mourning over a death
2 Samuel 12:15–17	David (seven days)	Pleading for a family member, for healing over illness
1 Kings 19:2–9	Elijah (forty days)	For physical strength, for traveling mercies
1 Kings 21:27	Wicked King Ahab (unknown duration, most likely one day)	Staving off disaster, intervention, and mercy
2 Chronicles 20:1–13	Jehoshaphat and the nation (unknown duration)	Staving off disaster, wisdom in what to do, and intervention, protection
Ezra 8:21–23	Ezra and the people (three days)	Traveling mercies, protection from danger
Ezra 10:6	Ezra (unknown duration)	Mourning over unfaithfulness
Nehemiah 1:4	Nehemiah (many days)	Mourning over a national disaster, wisdom in what to do
Nehemiah 9:1–2	The nation of Israel (one day)	Confession of sin
Esther 4:1–3	Mordecai, the Jews (unknown duration)	Intervention, staving off disaster
Esther 4:16	Esther and friends (three days)	Intervention, staving off disaster, and protection
Psalm 35:13	David (unknown duration)	For illness
Psalm 69:10–11	David (unknown duration)	Chastening the soul
Jeremiah 36:9	The nation of Israel (one day)	Confession of sin, staving off disaster, and mercy
Daniel 6:18 (NKJV)	The king (one evening)	Intervention
Daniel 9:3	Daniel (unknown duration)	Intervention, confession of sin
Daniel 10:2	Daniel (twenty-one days)	Wisdom, mourning, and in preparation for receiving
Joel 1:14, 2:12, 15	The nation of Israel (unknown duration)	Intervention, staving off disaster, confession, and mercy
Jonah 3:5	Pagan nation, the Ninevites (unknown duration)	Intervention, staving off disaster, and mercy
Matthew 4:2	Jesus (forty days)	In preparation for ministry
Matthew 6:16–18	Jesus's discourse	General fasting principles
Matthew 9:15	Jesus's discourse	Unknown purposes
Mark 9:29 (NKJV)	Jesus	Overcoming demonic strongholds

Luke 2:37	Anna (ongoing)	During Christian service, worshipping, and praying
Acts 9:9	Paul (three days)	Wisdom, intervention, for healing over illness, and in preparation for ministry
Acts 10:30–31 (NKJV)	Cornelius (four days)	Worshipping the Lord
Acts 13:2–3	Church leadership and workers (unknown duration)	Worshipping the Lord, setting apart of Christian workers, and in preparation for ministry
Acts 14:23	Paul and Barnabas (unknown duration)	Setting apart of Christian workers, in preparation for ministry
2 Corinthians 6:5 (NKJV)	Paul (unknown duration)	Many different reasons
2 Corinthians 11:27 (NKJV)	Paul (unknown duration)	For Christian work

EXAMPLES OF FASTING PROBLEMS, WRONG MOTIVES, OR ISSUES

Reference	Who	Issues
1 Kings 13:8–25	Prophet who was later eaten by a lion	Deceit, disobedience, and death
1 Kings 21:6–14	Jezebel	Wrong and sinful motives, death
Isaiah 58:3–4	The nation of Israel	Quarreling and strife
Luke 18:9–13	Pharisees	Pride, showmanship
Acts 23:12–15	Jews who wanted to assassinate Paul	Wrong and sinful motives, murder in their hearts

Arthur Wallis, in his book *God's Chosen Fast*, states the following:

Some of the great saints of church history have practiced fasting and testified to its value, among them the great Reformers, such as Luther, Calvin and Knox. The custom has not been confined to any theological school. Here we find Jonathan Edwards, the Calvinist, joining hands with John Wesley, the Arminian; and David Brainerd having fellowship with Charles Finney.[7]

In his book *Fasting for Spiritual Breakthroughs*, Elmer Towns adds the following:

In the early eighteenth century, the great evangelist Jonathan Edwards fasted for 24 hours before preaching the sermon many claim sparked the revival in New England that grew into the First

Great Awakening. The sermon was called "Sinners in the Hands of an Angry God"...A prayer revival swept throughout the nation in 1859, and some of it grew out of what might be called a type of fasting, because people did go without food. The revival began in the great metropolitan cities of the eastern United States. Christians left their work at noon, walked quickly to the nearest churches—not the churches of their memberships—and spent their lunch breaks in prayer.[8]

What Are the Purposes of a Fast?

As listed below, there are twenty-one different purposes of fasts.

Purposes of Fasts

1. Bearing children: 1 Samuel 1:6–18
2. Breaking down strongholds: Isaiah 58
3. Confession of sin—personally, corporately, or nationally: 1 Samuel 7:2–6, Nehemiah 9:1–2, Jeremiah 36:9, Daniel 9:3, Joel 1:14, Joel 2:12, 15
4. For healing of illness: 2 Samuel 12:15–17, Psalm 35:13, Acts 9:9
5. For physical strength to complete a task: 1 Kings 19:2–9
6. In preparation for a revelation or receiving something from God: Daniel 10:2, Acts 10:30–31
7. In preparation for ministry: Matthew 4:2, Acts 9:9, Acts 13:2–3, Acts 14:23
8. In service during kingdom work: Exodus 34:27–28, Luke 2:37
9. Intervention from the Almighty in a particular situation that you are facing: Judge 20:18–28, 1 Samuel 1:6–18, 1 Kings 21:27, 2 Chron. 20:1–13, Esther 4:1–3, 16, Daniel 6:18, Daniel 9:3, Joel 1:14, Joel 2:12, 15, Jonah 3:5, Acts 9:9
10. Mercy: Jeremiah 36:9, Joel 1:14, Joel 2:12, 15, Jonah 3:5

11. Mourning over national disaster: Nehemiah 1:14, Daniel 10:2
12. Mourning over sinfulness or the death of a family member, friend, or national leader: 1 Samuel 31:13, 2 Samuel 1:12, 2 Samuel 3:30–35, Ezra 10:6
13. Overcoming demonic strongholds: Mark 9:29
14. Pleading for a family member: 2 Samuel 12:15–17
15. Private affliction: 1 Samuel 1:6–18
16. Protection from danger: 2 Chron. 20:1–13, Ezra 8:21–23, Esther 4:16
17. Setting apart Christian workers: Acts 13:2–3, Acts 14:23
18. Staving off disaster—seen or unseen, personal or national: Judges 20:18–28, 1 Kings 21:27, 2 Chron. 20:1–13, Esther 4:1–3, 16, Jeremiah 36:9, Joel 1:14, Joel 2:12, 15, Jonah 3:5
19. Traveling mercies: 1 King 19:2–9, Ezra 8:21–23
20. Wisdom about what to do in a particular situation: Judges 20:18–28, 2 Chron. 20:1–13, Nehemiah 1:4, Daniel 10:2, Act 9:9
21. Worshipping the Lord: Luke 2:37, Acts 10:30–31, Acts 13:2–3

Towns continues to add:

Results that may be realized through fasting include (1) increased spiritual authority, (2) receiving divine affirmation of ministry, (3) obtaining new directions for the ministry, (4) gaining new insights during a Bible study that become foundational for ministry, (5) an enhanced desire to pray, (6) affirmation through the "sense of destiny" experiences, (7) new power for spiritual warfare, (8) guidance and liberty for workers in ministry, (9) victory over satanic strongholds, (10) assurance of divine protection, (11) an increased sense of God's presence, (12) a breaking of attitudes and policies hindering progress in a new ministry, and (13) times when prayer becomes enhanced as a means of effective wrestling with issues.[9]

What Are the Lengths of Bible Fasts?

In his sermon *Fasting Without Hypocrisy, Part 1*, John MacArthur, pastor of Grace Community Church in Sun Valley, California, says, "Listen, the Bible never prescribes the time for a fast; never. The time depends on the person, depends on the circumstances, depends on the situation, and the need."[10] I will add two more to that list: the movement of God and the expediency of the need.

How long you should fast is a personal issue between you and the Holy Spirit. There is no set time in the Bible for how long you are to fast. In the Bible, during the Day of Atonement, the Israelite nation was required to fast one day, from sunset to sunset. In Judges 20:26 it says, "They fasted that day until evening." Esther and Mordecai fasted three days, the men of Jabesh Gilead fasted seven days, Daniel fasted twenty-one days, and Moses, Elijah and Jesus fasted forty days. Some scholars go so far as to say that Moses fasted for eighty days at one time, based on Deuteronomy 9:9, 18. The length of a fast is a decision one needs to make according to the leading of the Holy Spirit. Jesus assumed that we would fast. However, even Jesus never prescribed the length of a fast.

If you are new to fasting, I would suggest you start fasting two meals a day, once a week, for three months. Start out slowly, using wisdom and discernment in listening to that still, small voice. Once you feel comfortable with fasting two meals a day, prayerfully consider bumping that up to three meals a day, once per week. After that, listen to the Holy Spirit and His instructions for you in your quiet times. You may be led to schedule a three-day fast later on in the year. In preparation for fasting, pray daily, journal, listen to that still, small voice, and determine to read your Bible regularly.

Why Do We Fast?

In Joel 2:12 the Bible says, "return to me with all your heart, with fasting and weeping and mourning." Fasting is certainly a means to express our innermost desire for the things of God; our being sold out for His causes. Fasting is an attempt to seek God and the things of God with the whole body, mind, and soul. Fasting is a natural outgrowth of focusing on the things of God.

In Leviticus 16:29, the Bible says, "*This* shall be a statute forever for you: In the seventh month, on the tenth *day* of the month, you shall <u>afflict</u> your souls, and do no work at all, *whether* a native of your own country or a stranger who dwells among you" (NKJV, emphasis added). As noted in a previous section of this book ("Is Fasting Ever Commanded in the Bible"), this verse pertains to the Day of Atonement—the only fasting day prescribed by God. In other versions of the Bible, "afflict your souls" is transcribed as "humbling your souls."

However, the fact that the Bible says we are to "afflict our souls" means something more than just going without food. Our bodies need food in order to be sustained. This verse about afflicting the soul tells us that the spiritual discipline of fasting impacts not only the body but also the soul. This illustrates an important lesson in the power of fasting. Some scholars conclude that the Hebrew mind of the Old Testament believed fasting allowed the soul to participate. I have experienced this in my fasts, which I attempted to explain in the sections titled "Heaven Came Down" and "Heaven Falls." It is hard to convey a spiritual event through words on paper, but during my fasts (as I wrote earlier), I felt as if I'd had a glimpse of eternity.

Towns, in his book, quotes Arthur Blessitt:

In my personal life, fasting has been for specific purposes and for a long duration. After three days, there are no hunger pains or desire for food. From twelve to fourteen days later, there seems to be a sense of complete cleanliness and mental clarity. After twenty-one days, there seems to be an *outpouring* of spiritual power and creativity that is *indescribable,* but that continues until the fast is ended. It seems especially after the third week that one is no longer even remotely interested in the trivial physical world around. One's mind is filled exclusively with profound spiritual ideas and truths...there is no question that there is awesome power in fasting.

If the fast is controlled by the Holy Spirit and Jesus is foremost, then it is a beautiful and powerful experience.[11] (Emphasis added.)

This is a key concept: fasting is something in which the soul participates! John Piper, in his book *A Hunger for God*, encapsulates everything in these words:

> The more deeply you walk with Christ, the hungrier you get *for* Christ...the more homesick you get for heaven...the more you want "all the fullness of God"...the more you want to be done with sin...the more you want the bridegroom to come...the more you want the church revived and purified with the beauty of Jesus... the more you want a great awakening to God's reality in the cities...the more you want to see the light of the Gospel of the glory of Christ penetrate the darkness of all the unreached peoples of the world...the more you want to see false worldviews yield to the force of Truth...the more you want to see pain relieved and tears wiped away and death destroyed...the more you long for every wrong to be made right and the justice and grace of God to fill the earth like the waters cover the sea.[12]

Again Piper says, of the great orator Charles Spurgeon, "The London pastor from a century ago, said, 'Our seasons of fasting and prayer at the Tabernacle have been high days indeed; never has heaven's gate stood wider; never have our hearts been nearer the central Glory.'"[13]

That is why we fast!

Prayer is reaching out after the unseen; fasting is letting go of all that is seen and temporal. Fasting helps express, deepen, confirm the resolution that we are ready to sacrifice anything, even ourselves to attain what we seek for the kingdom of God.[14]

Andrew Murray

CHAPTER 9

What Does Isaiah 58 Mean?

THIS IS ONE of the most important chapters of this book. My brothers and sisters, please read and study this chapter with an open, joyful, and receiving heart!

We can't have a study on fasting without studying Isaiah chapter 58. This is where God spells out what fasting is and what fasting is not. Isaiah was God's man, he was His prophet, the mouthpiece of God. Isaiah, like most Old Testament prophets, had the very difficult job of calling out sin in the face of great persecution so that God's people would turn back to Him. In twelve short verses God outlines the proper way to fast.

In verses 1–3, the Bible says God's people whined to the Lord while they were fasting because they were not seeing any results. They were, in essence, asking why they were going through the trouble of fasting only to have nothing change. God answered by pointing out their sins, their acts of violence, et cetera. He laid out the example of fasting for them, as well as for generations to come. Fasting was not to be just a one-day change of behavior, but it was to result in a changed life and heart.

The following are four obstacles to God hearing their prayers through fasting:

1. They were seeking their own pleasure for the day, when they should have been in a spirit of prayer and humbleness (verse 3).
2. They were exploiting (oppressing) their laborers, when they should have been alleviating some of their burdens (verse 3).

3. They were causing strife and debate, when they should have been seeking peace, mercy, and grace (verse 4).
4. They were striking their fists in anger and violence, when they should have been making peace with their enemies (verse 4).

The Bible then goes on to say, in verse 4, "You cannot fast as you do today and expect your voice to be heard on high." In other words, the Lord was answering the two questions they asked in verse 3 as to why their fasting prayers were not being heard. These four obstacles to fasting can be either outward actions or inward thoughts. Fasting with these obstacles in your life will cause your fasting to be completely in vain. It is nothing—worthless—according to the Lord. In his paper on fasting, Bob Jordan, chairman of the board for Prisoners For Christ, says,

Very few Christians really have an idea of how horrible and terrible sin is in the sight of a Holy God. We compare ourselves to others, and conclude we are not all that bad. Then we come to church and look forward to singing and hearing the preaching of the Word of God. In the Old Testament, the people wanted to hear from God, and to be blessed by God, but they were living in sin and weren't doing much about it. Fasting humbles the body and the soul and brings awareness of God's presence in a *manner unlike any other*. Christians who do not fast miss this opportunity of drawing near to God and hearing His voice.[15] (Emphasis added.)

Israel would fast, but as indicated in the Bible, they would continue to do whatever pleased them. Furthermore during the fasting time they continued to be mean and cruel to one another. Then they would expect God to bless them! This is not the kind of fasting God is looking for! The people were good at bowing down and looking outwardly like they were seeking God, but it was all form and ritual. God is interested in the heart of a man, not whether or not he is physically bowing down.[16]

The New Matthew Henry Commentary states,

> The true reason why God did not accept their fasting or answer the prayers they made on their fasts days: that they did not fast rightly. It was true they fasted, but they did not, like the Ninevites, turn away from their evil ways; they went on to *find pleasure* that is, to do whatever seemed right in their own eyes and pleased them, making their own inclinations fit their interpretation of the law... you must not only refrain from practicing wrong but also put to death in you every inclination toward it.[17]

That is the tough part—turning off our minds. Scripture says in Romans 12:2 to be "transformed by the renewing of your mind."

In Isaiah 58:6–7, God lays out what He expects of us when we fast—not just for the day but for a lifetime of fasting. In essence, we are to do exactly what they were *not* doing.

1. "Loose the chains of injustice."
2. "Untie the cords of the yoke."
3. "Set the oppressed free."
4. "Break every yoke."
5. "Share your food with the hungry."
6. "Provide the poor wanderer with shelter" (show hospitality to the poor or to strangers).
7. "When you see the naked, to clothe him."
8. "Not to turn away from your own flesh and blood" (provide for our own families, immediate as well as extended).

In their online article "Christian Fasting—Spiritual Growth," the folks at AllAboutGod.com write,

> Christian fasting is more than denying ourselves food or something else of the flesh—it's a *sacrificial lifestyle* before God. In

Isaiah 58, we learn what a "true fast" is. It's not just a one-time act of humility and denial before God, it's a *lifestyle of servant ministry* to others. As Isaiah tells us fasting encourages humility, loosens the chains of injustice, unties the cords of the yoke, frees the oppressed, feeds the hungry, provides for the poor and clothes the naked. This concept of fasting isn't a one day thing—it's a lifestyle of a servant living for God and others.[18] (Emphasis added.)

However, God did not just set forth guidelines for our fasting. In Isaiah 58:8–11, He also revealed some promises relating to our obedience.

Promise One: "Then your light will break forth like the dawn" (verse 8).

Promise Two: "Your healing will quickly appear" (verse 8).

Promise Three: "Your righteousness will go before you" (verse 8).

Promise Four: "The glory of the Lord will be your rear guard" (verse 8).

Promise Five: "Then you will call, and the Lord will answer" (verse 9).

Promise Six: "You will cry for help, and he will say: 'Here I am'" (verse 9).

Promise Seven: "Your light will rise in the darkness" (verse 10).

Promise Eight: "Your night will become like the noonday" (verse 10).

Promise Nine: "The Lord will guide you always" (verse 11).

Promise Ten: "He will satisfy your needs in a sun-scorched land" (verse 11).

Promise Eleven: "[He] will strengthen your frame" (verse 11).

Promise Twelve: "You will be like a well-watered garden, like a spring whose waters never fail" (verse 11).

As I meditated on these promises, I realized there was not one of them I would not want in *abundance* for the rest of my life! What Christian would not want just one or two of these promises fulfilled in his or her lifetime? I desire to have all twelve of these promises in my life for the remaining years that I walk this earth. I would love to have the Lord be my rear guard, watching my back at all times—things that I can see and things I can't see.

I would love to have the Lord guide me continually or to have the Lord answer me when I call or to satisfy my soul in times of drought or to strengthen my bones or to refresh me like a well-watered garden. A discussion of these twelve promises could fill the space of an entire book.

The Almighty, who created the universe, has promised these twelve things when we fast with the right motives. He is faithful, and His promises are always true. Wherever there is a biblical promise, there will always be some type of stipulation. If I desire the favor of the Almighty with these twelve promises, it would be smart for me to study the things that would prevent me from receiving them—the four items listed in verses 3 and 4. It would also benefit me to study the eight stipulations found in verses 6 and 7.

Some folks reading this might think I was striving, through good works, to obtain blessings from the Lord. Wrong! It is not about works; it is about faith and understanding the totality of God's Word concerning His promises for His children. I have a heartfelt desire for the things of God! If I desire the things of God, then I should desire to remove any obstacles and replace them with the things that please God. The Bible instructs us to become more Christlike, to be imitators of God. In our journey through life, we should study the things that please God and attempt to excel in those areas.

I would encourage you to take one of God's prerequisites found in verses 6 and 7 (I will list them again) each month, study and meditate on it, and then attempt to put it into practice in your everyday life.

1. "Loose the chains of injustice."
2. "Untie the cords of the yoke."
3. "Set the oppressed free."

4. "Break every yoke."
5. "Share your food with the hungry."
6. "Provide the poor wanderer with shelter."
7. "When you see the naked, to clothe him."
8. "Not to turn away from your own flesh and blood."

§

The House Sale: A Personal Testimony

Being a student of fasting, I have read Isaiah 58 multiple times. It wasn't until Rhonda and I decided to downsize and sell our house in 2014 that the full ramifications of the Isaiah passage fell into place.

Rhonda and I lived in our house in Duvall for fifteen years. It was a two-story home, and as we were continuing to march down the aging path, we decided it was time to think about downsizing. We sat down with pen in hand and wrote out our "must-haves," as well as a list of "our wants." As husband and wife, we took our desires before the Lord and were unified that it was the right time to make a move. So we first embarked on a house search. We must have looked at twenty-five to thirty homes over the course of several months. Nothing seemed to meet our needs.

One day Rhonda came into my office and said, "I think I have found the right house, but we may need to act quickly." Just what I wanted to hear—"act quickly." As I have mentioned, I am not a spur-of-the-moment type of guy. I don't like to act quickly on big-ticket items. I don't want to feel pressured. So when I heard her words, I mentally rolled my eyes, thinking we had already been priced out of the market of anything we could afford. I was frustrated but didn't want to show that frustration to my bubbly wife. I agreed to go with her after work to preview the house she had found.

Guess what—much to my pleasant surprise, this was *the* house for the Von Tobels. Everything we had placed on our list of "must-haves," as well as "our wants," was wrapped up in this one house. I was excited. Rhonda was excited. We were ready to take action. We engaged the realtors that we had used over the last twenty years, Joe and Marcea Galindo, and we were off and running. We had heard from others who had recently sold their homes that the market was sizzling hot and that some houses were entertaining multiple offers. We made an offer on the new house on the contingency of selling our current one. This was the first part of October 2014.

For all major decisions, I fast. I decided to do a three-day fast. I placed our desires before the Lord. I was at peace in my heart knowing that if it was the Lord's will for us to sell, then it would happen. If it was not in His will, then it wouldn't happen.

The day we put our house on the market, the real-estate market came to a screeching halt—dead in the water. Days turned into weeks. Rhonda and I were hoping to be in our new house by Christmas of 2014. What we thought would be a quick sale (with multiple offers) never materialized. Thanksgiving came and went. We were now in what realtors call the "red zone" or the "zone of death"—that time between Thanksgiving and Christmas when very few houses sell. Yes, some do sell, but most house buying and selling activity comes to a standstill. Rhonda and I finally came to a realization that our house was not going to sell and that we wouldn't get *the* house. *Sigh.* We were at peace. We never asked why this happened; we just knew in our hearts it wasn't meant to be. Having fasted gave me even greater peace.

We decided on a Friday that we would take the house off the market the following Monday and relist it in the spring. This decision would ultimately seal our fate of not getting the house that we so desired. We were truly at peace and ready to move on.

§

In the meantime, I was writing this book and going deeper into God's Word in Isaiah 58. I felt prompted to meditate on and search my heart about the stipulations that God had set forth regarding those who fast. I searched my heart, but I kept coming back to two of the eight items: undoing the heavy burdens and providing for your own flesh. This perplexed me. What exactly did this mean, and why was I coming back to these two requirements? I first thought the two were unrelated ideas that the Holy Spirit wanted me to reflect on and consider more deeply. I examined my heart again but really didn't come up with anything that needed to be corrected in my life...until one day the Holy Spirit revealed to me what needed to be done.

In 2009, I'd had some family members come to me needing a bridge loan. It wasn't a significant amount of money; it wouldn't put us in the poorhouse if we didn't get paid back. However, they agreed that their budget would allow them to pay it back in a timely fashion. The recession was deep, jobs were lost, and payments weren't made. It was a burden for them as it was for me. It was awkward.

Fast-forward five years, and the Holy Spirit is nudging me to release them from this burden. Not being a man of wealth, I believed I needed to be a good steward of what the Lord had entrusted to me. Nevertheless, the Holy Spirit instructed me to forgive the outstanding balance. I was reminded that the Lord is able to do *abundantly and exceedingly* more than what I could ever anticipate. I knew this in my heart, but it was time to put it into practice. I agreed in my spirit this was the right thing to do. I filed it away as a discussion point for when Rhonda and I would have a chance to sit down and talk.

§

As I shared earlier, we made the decision on a Friday to delist our house the following Monday. I decided to take Rhonda out to a nice dinner Monday night to discuss our plan for relisting the house in the spring. All that day I received phones calls from realtor after realtor who wanted to relist our house—all of them promised a quick sale. It was nauseating to listen to their spiels. Rhonda and I were halfway through our meal when I told her that I was feeling led by the Holy Spirit to release our family members from the liability of the loan. She was in full agreement. Now that my wife was on board with the decision, I felt at peace.

Minutes after Rhonda and I had agreed to undo the heavy burden of the loan, I received a call on my cell phone. I told Rhonda that all day long I had been receiving calls from realtors who wanted to relist our house. I wasn't going to take this call, but I felt prompted to do so. The number on the caller ID led me to believe it was another realtor, and sure enough, it was. I told the caller that the house had been taken off the market that very day, that it was no longer for sale, and that we were going to relist it in the spring.

There was a long pause before she responded, "Mr. Von Tobel, I have a party who is really interested in your home."

I responded, in my most snarky of tones, "And all the realtors who are calling me today are guaranteeing a quick sale as well."

There was another long pause before she replied, "Mr. Von Tobel, you don't understand. I *do* have an interested party, and I would like to show your house tomorrow. And what's more, she is an all-cash buyer." At the words "all-cash buyer," she now had my undivided attention.

I told her that the lockbox had been taken off the front door and that the for-sale sign was coming down. I went on to tell her that if she truly had a buyer, she would have twenty-four hours to put something together. Otherwise, I planned to forget about the house for a while and move into the Christmas spirit.

That was Monday night around eight o'clock. The Tuesday house showing happened as promised. Wednesday we had an offer in our hands, and by Thursday, we had sold our house. Still, that was only part of the equation. On the same Monday that we decided to delist our house, I'd also had to make that dreaded call to the other realtor to rescind our offer to the contractor who had *the* house we wanted. On Wednesday morning, I had to call the realtor again to say that we were back in the game. I was treated to another long pause on the phone. My heart started pounding as the realtor said, "We have active buyers who are interested in the house. We are expecting an offer from them shortly." In the end, it turned out that those buyers blinked and hesitated just long enough for us to wrap up the details on our end, securing *the* house for us by God's providential hand of mercy.

From the time we delisted our old house to the day we were actually moving into our new home was an astounding turnaround of only thirty days.

Unheard of!

God had an all-important lesson for me to learn—that I am to live my life excelling in His requirements on fasting. Once Rhonda and I decided to undo the burdens of others, less than twenty minutes went by before we received the phone call that enabled us to buy the house we so desired. We have a God who wants to give His children good things. However, He does require something of us: obedience to His precepts.

What things in your personal life might be hindering God from fully opening the floodgates in answer to your prayer requests? What are the mountains in your life that need to be blown away? Is it something found in those eight prerequisites of Isaiah 58? Is it unforgiveness? Do you need to make amends with a friend or a family member, regardless of who is at fault? Does your thought life need to be cleaned up? Do you have an anger problem in your mind? Do you obsess over how you have been mistreated at the office? Have you been wronged, and are you fixating on how you might read someone the riot act? Do you think more highly of yourself than you should? Do you have issues with a neighbor that need resolution? Is there something between you and a business partner that needs to be made new?

Reflect on those questions, and make concerted strides toward eliminating anything that would prevent God from being your rear guard.

If pride is the epidemic vice, then humility is the endangered virtue. Humility is so rare because it is unnatural to man.[19]

Stuart Scott

CHAPTER 10

What Does Jesus Say about Fasting?

WHAT DID JESUS have to say about fasting? I believe it is important to correlate any principles of the Old Testament with those of the New Testament. Jesus had a lot to say about fasting—positive as well as negative. In this chapter, we are going to look at a number of scriptures dealing with Jesus's teaching on fasting.

Matthew 6:2-18

Matthew 6:2–18 is a very interesting set of scriptures. In these verses, Jesus takes the opportunity to bring to light three pharisaical practices that He condemned. In verse 2, it reads, "So when you give to the needy, do not announce it with trumpets, as the hypocrites do." Here, Jesus is speaking against the pride and showmanship of the Pharisees. He is setting the standard that we are to give in secret so no one knows what we give. Out of His love for us, this guidance is a protection for us from the sin of pride and self-righteousness taking hold in our lives. If we follow this rule of confidentiality, it will help keep us from the devil's schemes and entanglements. It will protect us from conceit and arrogance.

In verse 4, Jesus says, "Then your Father, who sees what is done in secret, will reward you." I don't know about you, but I certainly want to find favor with the Almighty and receive His rewards.

Verse 5 starts out the same way when Jesus says, "And when you pray, do not be like the hypocrites, for they love to pray standing in the synagogues and on the street corners to be seen by men. I tell you the truth, they have received their reward in full. But when you pray, go into your room, close the door and pray to your Father who is unseen." Jesus is once again setting the standard. He wants us to pray in private. He is not speaking against those who pray corporately or in prayer circles, but against those who pray to show off their piety.

Near the middle of this discourse, in verse 6, Jesus says, "Then your Father, who sees what is done in secret, will reward you." Again, I desire the things of the Lord and want to find favor with Him. I don't think there is a Bible-believing Christian who does not want to receive rewards from the Father while on this earth. Yes, our true rewards are in heaven, but it is also nice to receive earthly rewards and blessings.

Jesus takes it to another level when, in verse 16, He says, "When you *fast*, do not look somber as the hypocrites do, for they disfigure their faces to show men they are fasting" (emphasis added). Jesus again tells us to do things in private. Jesus says that we are to do the exact opposite of what the Pharisees were doing. He says we are to put oil on our heads and wash our faces; in other words, we are to look refreshed. Jesus closes out this teaching on fasting with "...and your Father, who sees what is done in secret, will reward you."

New Life Community Church, in its article on biblical fasting, adds even greater insight to this hypocrisy that Jesus speaks against:

By Jesus' time fasting had become a very important part of the Jewish life. Perhaps *overly* important would be a better way to say it. Based on Luke 18:2a, we know the Pharisees fasted twice a week. The Talmud tells us that this was on the 2nd and 5th day (Monday and Thursday). Why those days? According to the Pharisees it was because Moses went up on Mt. Sinai to get the Law on the 5th day and returned on the 2nd. At least that's what they said.

But if you look closely into the Jewish history, you find another possible reason for the Pharisees fasting on Monday and Thursday. Market day in the city of Jerusalem was on the 2nd and 5th day! Everyone from the countryside came to town on those days. It was on these two days that the Pharisees chose to hold their fasts. They would walk through the streets with their hair disheveled; they would put on old clothes and cover themselves with dirt; they would cover their faces with white chalk in order to look pale; and they would dump ashes over their head as a sign of their humility!! Fasting had become a "look-at-how-spiritual-I-am" exercise. It was hypocrisy.

Biblical fasting is not hypocrisy. It is not a manipulative tool. It is not a physical discipline.[20]

However, Bill Bright, the late founder and CEO of Campus Crusade for Christ, in his book *The Transforming Power of Fasting and Prayer*, gives some further insight when he writes,

Many people are reluctant to tell others that they are fasting so they will avoid the sin that the Pharisees committed—fasting just to gain recognition. I strongly believe, however, that it is a trick of the enemy to keep our fasting a secret. By isolating ourselves from the support of other Christians, we may be more susceptible to doubts and negative influences (both human and demonic). We need the prayer shield of our Christian friends and family members to help us continue when we feel alone and when the enemy tempts us to give up.[21]

Let's analyze these verses in Matthew 6 further. Jesus starts out each segment of His discourse with "when": *when* you give, *when* you pray, *when* you fast. He didn't say *if* you give or *if* you pray, and He certainly did not say *if* you fast. There were no "ifs" in His teaching. He said *when* you do these things. He was not *commanding* us to do these things; He was assuming that we would do them as a natural outgrowth of our faith. Jesus never instructed His followers on the length of a fast or the frequency of fasting.

Believers, for the most part, understand that they are to give. They even understand that they are to pray. Why, then, don't they understand that they are to fast? This is a complex issue. Richard Foster, in his classic book *Celebration of Discipline*, reveals a startling discovery: "For example, in my research I could not find a single book published on the subject of Christian fasting from 1861 to 1954, a period of nearly one hundred years. More recently a renewed interest in fasting has developed, but we have far to go to recover a biblical balance."[22]

Briefly, there are four reasons why the modern-day American believer does not grasp the importance of fasting.

1. *Lack of "pulpit-pounding" messages on fasting.* When I first became a believer in Christ, tithing was a *pulpit-pounding* message that I heard—not just once, but multiple times. In the early years of my new walk with the Lord, we were constantly being challenged to give financially to kingdom work. When I first became a believer in Christ in 1982, I was a miser. Pure and simple, I didn't give. I was tight-fisted with whatever money I had under my control, which wasn't much at the time. I certainly didn't understand the phrase going around Christendom at that time: "Give until it hurts!" Give until it hurts…really? What genius thought of that catchphrase? That was a nonmotivator to say the least!

   It took almost five years into my Christian walk before I embraced giving. (I was a slow learner.) It wasn't until my pastor, Bob Moorehead, made a statement in one of his sermons that finally shocked me into reality. He said, "You are either going to give your money to the kingdom of God or you are going to give it to the kingdom of Satan in the form of mechanical breakdowns, surprise bills, car repairs, or medical bills. You make the choice; who are you going to give it to?"

That captured my attention. As I was trying to digest that news, he leveled me once again with a blast right between the eyes. "For the next six months, if you will tithe the full ten percent to the church, and if at the end of the six months you can come to me and say you are no better off than you were before you started, this church will pay you back everything you tithed in the last six months." Huh? Really? What a statement! I planned to take him up on that deal. Guess what? Rhonda and I have been tithing ever since. We haven't looked back once, working to excel in our giving. I finally got it! It is now a joy to give. As men, sometimes we need a direct, hard-hitting challenge. That is what it took for me. In the same way, believers in Christ often need to be challenged in order to learn the discipline of fasting.

Over the years I have heard many "pulpit-pounding" messages on both tithing and prayer. However, in my thirty-two years as a Christian, I have heard only two messages on fasting in my entire walk with the Lord. We need to hear more of these messages from our churches. This leads me to my next point.

2. *Lack of teaching in new members and discipleship classes.* I often get together for lunch with my good friend Bob Jordan. We are birds of a feather—iron sharpening iron. Most of the time, we think very much alike. We discuss a variety of subjects during our lunches together, but we always return to our favorite topics of evangelism and discipleship. We lament both because of what we see and don't see in our local churches. The Bible was meant to transform our culture, but in today's environment, we find our culture attempting to transform the teachings of the Bible. Why? The era of the seeker-friendly movement has ravaged our churches to the point of rendering them impotent. In 2 Timothy 4:3, Paul writes, "For the time will come when men will not put up with sound doctrine. Instead, to suit their own desires, they will gather around them a great number of teachers to say what their itching ears want to hear."

Churches are not producing what they have been called to produce—disciples of Jesus, imitators of Christ. I believe we are living in the end times and that the Lord's return is imminent. If that truly is the case, why do we have so many churches not equipping the saints or even sensing the urgency? Men and women of God are woefully undereducated in the basic tenets and doctrines of their faith.

There are many good churches with discipleship material. My church, Canyon Hill Community Church, has the School of Discipleship. In the Sunday bulletin insert introducing the fall 2015 schedule, the school was teaching three different classes: Survey of Theology 2, Pseudo-Christian Cults and Views, and the Foundations Class. The description of that Foundations course reads as follows: "This 8-week, general survey class covers the foundational doctrines of the church. This class will include such topics as the inerrancy of Scripture, the doctrine of sin, and spiritual disciplines. This is a great class for new Christians or for the seasoned believer who is looking for a refresher course in the core doctrines of the Christian faith."

My aforementioned friend, Bob Jordan, is teaching a class at his church, Cedar Park Assembly of God. The description of that course reads as follows: "After attending this one-year course, you will be a dangerous Christian, dangerous to the enemy! Much teaching and interaction, fast paced, fun, informative, practical, designed for any believer but especially for those who are new Christians. This class brings a truly unique approach of going through the Bible in one year and is guaranteed to radically affect your Christian walk! This course is designed for new believers but is applicable and useful to all levels of Christian maturity."

We are called to make disciples, teaching believers the things of God. We can do that one-on-one or in a classroom. If we do not teach new believers the things instructed in the Bible, we are facilitating spiritual desertion—birthing them and abandoning them for the wolves to devour. We must teach new believers how to pray, how to give, and how to fast.

3. ***Our prosperity is a hindrance.*** For the most part, in the evangelical church, we understand the concept of giving and praying. It is easy to give; it is easy to pray. It is not, however, easy to fast. Therein lies the rub for the American believer. We don't like pain. We don't like to do without. Because of our prosperity and the ability to solve our problems on our own, we don't need to rely on God to come to our aid. We believe we can fix it ourselves. This is the dark side to the entrepreneurial spirit and capitalistic society in which we live.

I believe one of the greatest tools that Satan has used to render the American believers' faith ineffective is the credit card and the line of credit on our homes. When the furnace breaks, when the transmission goes out in our cars, when one of our family members needs to go to the hospital, when we need to send one of our kids to college, or even when a family pet needs medical attention…what do we do? We immediately pull out the plastic and pay for it without any prayer or fasting. No questions asked. It has to get done. We just solve our own problems.

Is this what God wants from us? Do we first inquire of God? Most likely not! Often we find ourselves in this vicious cycle of continuing to increase our monthly expenditures, leaving less and less disposable income that we could use to build up the kingdom of God. Some go so far as to pile debt upon debt upon debt until the debt load is crushing. We never ask the Lord what we are to do, and one bad decision leads to another. What kind of insanity is that?

At some point, even believers under the mounds of debt file for bankruptcy—all because they didn't slow down and stop to inquire of the Lord. Do you know what is done in other cultures when people can't pay their bills? They are thrown into debtors' prison! I have seen it firsthand as we stood waiting to go into a church service in a foreign prison. I look up at the chalkboard where the demographics of the prison are listed, and sure enough, there are listings for debtor inmates!

When these things happen to our Christian brothers and sisters in different cultures, what do they do? They go to their knees, they pray, they fast, they inquire of the Lord...and then they wait. This is not normally the case for the American believer. Jesus asks the question in Luke 18:8: "When the Son of Man comes, will he find faith on earth?" Foster sums it up with this statement:

> Why has the giving of money, for example, been unquestionably recognized as an element in Christian devotion and fasting so disputed? Certainly we have as much, if not more, evidence from the Bible for fasting as we have for giving. Perhaps in our affluent society fasting involves a far larger sacrifice than the giving of money.[23]

4. *The American church has not gone through persecution yet.* Throughout the world, Christians are being killed daily. The universal church is under immense persecution. Missiologists, who study persecution, tell us that when there is such oppression in other lands, those who are being persecuted are crying out to the Almighty in prayer and fasting. History has shown us that when severe persecution occurs, the church really takes root and takes off.

The American church has not seen severe persecution in our history as a nation. Why? I believe it is for two reasons. First, because the founding fathers of this country based their principles of government on faith in the Almighty. And second, because until now, we have been a defender of Israel. In Numbers 24:9, God says, "May those who bless you [Israel] be blessed and those who curse you be cursed!" Dark is the day that this country turns its back on Israel!

As I have discussed, in Matthew 6:2–18, Jesus said "when" you do these things—when you give, when you pray, and when you fast. He didn't say "if" you do these things. He also said that when you do these things with the proper motives of the heart, and in private, that our Father in heaven would reward you. My dear brothers and sisters in the Lord, in my past life I strove to provide good things for my family. It wasn't until I stopped striving, instead doing things God's way and in God's time, that spiritual rewards started flowing into my life. But my motivation to do things God's way is not to receive more! God's blessings aren't just in the form of finances but in many other ways as well.

However, there is a biblical truth in Matthew 6:33 when Jesus says, "But seek first his kingdom and his righteousness, and all these things will be given to you as well." It is so much more fun to be rewarded by the Father than to strive in life just to squeak by. This is neither about the prosperity movement nor the name-it-and-claim-it doctrine. It is all about receiving what God wants to give His children, according to His will. It is not about what we want to receive from God; it is about what He wants to give to us. I can guarantee, whatever He wants to give to you is so much better than what you want to receive by the works of your own hands.

Matthew 9:14-15

The Bible says, in Matthew 9:14,

> Then John's disciples came and asked Him, "How is it that we and the Pharisees fast, but your disciples do not fast?"
>
> Jesus answered, "How can the guests of the bridegroom mourn while he is with them? The time will come when the bridegroom will be taken from them; then they will fast."

This can be a very confusing scripture if you do not understand the context of the Jewish wedding day. Jesus answered them with a comparison to the bridegroom and their community culture of the wedding day. On the wedding day, when the bridegroom was present, there was no need for mourning. The wedding day was a celebratory time. It would be improper for any of the attendees on the day of the wedding to be in the spirit of mourning. The wedding day was a joyous occasion for the Jewish family and the local community. However, it was too early in His ministry for the disciples to understand His point. What Jesus was saying was that once He ascended into heaven to be with the Father, then His disciples would fast. Many theologians believe that Jesus was validating the spiritual discipline of fasting for the church age, in which we are living.

Mark 9:14-29

Here we have another example of Jesus's teaching on fasting. Jesus had just taken three of His disciples to the top of a mountain where He was trans-figured. Coming down from the mountain, Jesus saw a group of teachers of the law arguing with His disciples. It happened that a distraught father had approached the disciples to heal his son from demonic oppression. The father told Jesus that His disciples could not expel this evil spirit. Jesus then said, "O, unbelieving generation…how long shall I stay with you?" With that, Jesus expelled the demon.

Once Jesus and His disciples went indoors in private, the disciples in-quired of Jesus why they could not expel the demon. Jesus said to them in Mark 9:29, "This kind can come out by nothing but prayer and fasting" (NKJV). This incident of Jesus expelling a deaf, mute spirit teaches His disciples (and should teach us) a critical lesson about the coupling of fast-ing to prayer.

In Shansi I found Chinese Christians who were accustomed to spend time in fasting and prayer. They recognized that this fasting, which so many dislike, which requires faith in God, since it makes one feel weak and poorly, is really a Divinely appointed means of grace. Perhaps the greatest hindrance to our work is our own imagined strength; and in fasting we learn what poor, weak creatures we are—dependent on a meal of meat for the little strength which we are so apt to lean upon.[24]

Hudson Taylor

CHAPTER 11

Three Favorite Fasting Examples

I AM GOING to share with you three of my favorite Bible stories about fasting. It is always exciting to see how God used ordinary people to accomplish the extraordinary things for Him. In the next few pages we will journey deep into the Old Testament to focus on three of the most fascinating fasting stories ever written.

Jonah

Around 775 BC, Israel was in full rebellion against God with their stubborn hearts and their practice of idolatry. Throughout the Old Testament, the Lord would often chastise Israel for their sins. He would do this in the form of an army coming against them and taking them captive.

In this case, the army was coming from the north. They were called the Assyrians. The Assyrians were a cruel and ruthless people. They were an evil empire. They committed many atrocities and war crimes against their enemies. Just the name Assyria struck terror in the hearts of the Israelites. The Assyrians were a much-hated and dreaded enemy of Israel. The atrocities of the Assyrians were as notorious and well known as the atrocities we see perpetrated by the Islamic group ISIS. They were that brutal.

The Bible tells us that there was a man by the name of Amittai who lived at this time. He had a son he named Jonah. Some call Jonah "the reluctant evangelist"; others call him "the runaway evangelist." Jonah had a calling on his life to be God's mouthpiece. Many people who read the book of Jonah believe it is a book about a man and a fish, but it truly is not. It is about God's mercy and love for all of mankind. It is about God's message of salvation not being beyond the reach of anyone—even the inmate!

Growing up in this era, Jonah certainly would have known about the violence that the Assyrian nation had inflicted on their enemies. Jonah may even have known family members or friends who had been tortured and murdered by people of this nation. Jonah hated the Assyrians and didn't want them to repent because he knew God's love had no bounds. Jonah wanted God's wrath to fall on this barbaric nation, not His mercy. (Does this sound familiar?) However, God had a plan for Jonah's life, and it was to preach to this ruthless people a message of repentance for their sins. God said to Jonah "Go!" Instead of going, Jonah ran away to Joppa, a seaport city on the Mediterranean Sea.

For years, I judged Jonah for not getting it right the first time. When you are not in the heat of the battle, it is easy to judge. To put this in a way we can relate to today, it would be like God saying to Greg Von Tobel, "I want you to go to Mosul, Iraq, and speak out against ISIS. Go to their cities and their military outposts and preach against them." I am pretty sure my response would be, "Huh? Come again, God? I have heard of their atrocities. They are beheading people, killing children, raping women—and you want me to do *what*?" I have to admit, I too might be looking to hop the first boat to Hawaii. It would take a big fish to grab my attention as well.

The story goes on to say that Jonah boarded a ferry to Tarshish. Many theologians say Tarshish was in Spain almost 2,500 miles away. In other words, Jonah was attempting to run as far away from God as possible. A storm came up. Instead of repenting for his sin of disobedience, he told the sailors to throw him overboard. About ready to die, Jonah prayed what he thought was his last prayer. A great fish swallowed Jonah whole. While inside the belly of the fish, Jonah had a come-to-Jesus meeting, so to speak. He cried out to God for forgiveness, and miraculously, the big fish spit Jonah out onto dry land. Jonah got a second chance to get it right—a do-over, a mulligan. The Bible is unclear on how much time it took Jonah to travel, but the next stop was Nineveh, where Jonah finally got it right.

Nineveh was soon to be the capital city of those ruthless Assyrians. The Bible says it was a powerful but a wicked city. Being a prominent city of Assyria meant that Nineveh was a wealthy city as well. With wealth comes all the things that money buys—fine food, fine clothes, and fine homes. These were rich people, the aristocrats of society.

Jonah showed up in Nineveh. The first day on the job, he preached, "Forty more days and Nineveh will be overturned" (Jonah 3:4). The Bible says in the next verse, "The Ninevites believed God" (verse 5).

Excuse me? What? Let's stop for a moment to analyze this. Jonah shows up on his first day on the job, preaches eight words, "Forty more days and Nineveh will be overturned," and this pagan, horrific, evil nation—who did not know God—believed God! This is in stark contrast to the nation of Israel! God so loved His chosen people that He sent prophet after prophet after prophet to warn them of impending doom, and still they would not turn from their evil ways. Nineveh hears eight words and changes course immediately. Apart from the divine intervention of God, this repentance cannot be explained.

This was not a casual conversion of belief for the Ninevites. It was not just lip service. How do we know? We know because the Bible says in Jonah 3:5 they backed their belief with action. The next few verses say, "They declared a *fast*, and all of them, from the greatest to the least, put on sackcloth" (emphasis added). Sackcloth was a sign of mourning and typically meant submission. Some say sackcloth might have been made of goat's hair and was black. It was a form of humbling yourself before God. What did this nation of evildoers know about humbling themselves before God? Maybe they had seen this fasting discipline in some of their conquests, or maybe Jonah instructed them in what to do. We don't know, as the Bible is silent on this matter. However, we do know they believed and they fasted.

It is one thing for the commoners to act this way, but what about those wealthy aristocrats with the fine clothes? Did they put on sackcloth and ashes and sit in the dust? Let's see what the king of Nineveh did.

"When the news reached the king of Nineveh, he rose from his throne, took off his royal robes, covered himself with sackcloth and sat down in the dust" (Jonah 3:6). Sitting in the dust is another form of humbling oneself. "Then he issued a proclamation in Nineveh. [Personal action coupled with corporate action.] 'Do not let any man or beast, herd or flock, taste anything; do not let them eat or drink. But let man and beast be covered with sackcloth. Let *everyone* call *urgently* on God. Let them give up their evil ways and their violence. Who knows? God may yet *relent* and with *compassion* turn from his fierce anger so that we will not perish'" (Jonah 3:7–9, emphasis added).

He got it! He humbled himself in the sight of a mighty God. As leader of the nation, he took action; he called a fast. How did this evil ruler know about the power of a fast? Again, we don't really know. This pagan nation that didn't fear anything, on this occasion, feared God.

They did their part. And how did God respond? "When God saw what they did and how they turned from their evil ways, he had compassion and did not bring upon them the destruction he had threatened" (Jonah 3:10). Wow, what a plot twist!

The king of Nineveh called for a fast to *stave off disaster*. It was not just a personal fast but was what is called a corporate fast: calling a multitude of people to come together to implore God to relent for what He has already decreed.

Arthur Wallis, in his book *God's Chosen Fast*, declares, "Wherever in Scripture we read of a public emergency being met by a national call to fast, we find without exception that God responded in deliverance."[25]

§

As the leader of Prisoners For Christ, I have only called two corporate fasts in our history. Once when one of our PFC short-term mission's team's passports had not arrived from the Rwandan Embassy. The team was scheduled to board a plane for the other side of the world in just five days, and their passports had still not arrived. Once we determined how dire our need was, we devised a plan to send a member of the team, my friend Bob Jordan, on a flight from Seattle to San Francisco to personally pick up the passports at the embassy.

We had poured six months into planning the trip. Cancelling was not an option. Rescheduling our airline tickets would have been extremely costly. To make matters worse, we were making no headway with embassy staff, who could not locate our passports with the visas in them. It seemed as if the passports had slipped into a black hole—which was even worse than just being late. I called a three-day fast to intercede for our needs before God. Two days into the fast, the passports showed up in our mail, fully executed with visas. No one at the embassy could explain what had happened.

The second time I called a fast was many years ago over the financial affairs of the ministry. Anyone who has ever attempted to raise monies for a prison ministry knows firsthand, it is not an easy task. We don't have "poster kids" we can wave in front of the world. The people we serve have checkered pasts and pretty rough edges. It is hard sometimes, even within the Christian community, to raise awareness for the evangelistic need of this part of society. For many small nonprofits, it is always a struggle to meet payroll by the end of the month.

This particular month, we were nearly $20,000 short of covering all the monthly bills, including payroll. This was the most we had ever been short. It was summer, which is always the time when donations are extremely low. It was frightening. I was wringing my hands. I care deeply about our staff, and the thought of missing payroll was, quite frankly, very painful. All of our staff could be making way more money out in the private sector, but they chose to work here at PFC and use their skill sets for the furtherance of the kingdom.

Board meetings for PFC are always the third Thursday of every other month. The following week is always payroll week. I informed the board at the meeting that month that I didn't think we were going to make pay-roll. Being short on funds was *not* new waters for us, but the size of the deficit was. I called for a three-day fast. In the days that followed, we had a check for $15,000 walk into our office one day and multiple smaller sur-prise checks came through the mail, which matched our need for $20,000.

In times of trouble and in times of decision-making, leaders should not be afraid to call for a fast! What would our country be like if the lead-ers, from the president on down to Congress, would humble themselves and call a nationwide fast? The pagan king of Nineveh did it. We should have the courage to do so as well. Only humbleness saved Nineveh. Only humbleness can save America.

America is a country that has turned its back on God. America has greatly and unapologetically sinned against a holy and righteous God. Someone once said that America is a country that has forgotten how to blush. I agree with that statement wholeheartedly! Our Supreme Court has turned liberal, giving the thumbs-up on all sorts of abominations. America no longer fears God, and its people do as they please. If it wasn't for the steadfast hand of the Lord withholding His judgment and for the prayers of the remnant, we would have already turned into a pagan nation. Our only hope for the future is not in changing the guard in Washington, DC, but it is in prayer and fasting.

John MacArthur states it succinctly in his paper on biblical fasting:

The people of Nineveh believed God and proclaimed a fast. They poured out their hearts. They were afraid of the judgment of God. We don't have enough of that today. If you go around preaching the judgment of God, people get mad at you. And the people who get mad at you aren't the unsaved, they're the saved. They say you don't have any love. That somebody's going to die and perish and go to hell. I think the loving thing to do is to warn them, don't you? But we don't really care about the lost the way we should. When's the last time you skipped a meal because you were so exercised in your spirit over our nation which is condemned to hell without

Christ? Over our world? Over your neighbors? Over somebody you know and love? When's the last time you had a sense of condemnation, the urgency of anxiety over doom that's going to come to those without God?[26]

Esther

This story takes place around 480 BC. It tells about Esther, also known as Hadassah, who was an orphan adopted by her cousin Mordecai. Esther became queen and ultimately saved her people from annihilation. Once again God used an evil nation, the Babylonians, as a tool to chasten the nation of Israel for their sin of idolatry by taking them into captivity.

In the city of Susa, King Xerxes was the reigning king, married to Queen Vashti. Through a set of circumstances, the queen fell out of favor with the king. After consulting with his advisors, the king decreed "that Vashti [was] never again to enter the presence of King Xerxes" (Esther 1:19). The king's officials scoured the countryside for maidens who might be suitable to be the new queen. Esther was chosen because of her beauty and became King Xerxes's queen. Esther was ordered by her cousin Mordecai to keep her Jewish nationality a secret.

There was also a king's official by the name of Haman who, because of pride, was bent on evil. He was a proud man and very jealous of Mordecai because Mordecai would not bow down to him at the city gates. Haman plotted to kill Mordecai as well as all the Jews throughout "all of the king's provinces" (Esther 3:13). His plan was one of a mass genocide of the Jews in their country. Haman manipulated the king into issuing an edict to kill all of the Jews in the region. This edict was sealed by the king's signet ring. The king gave his ring to Haman as a promise that his order to eradicate the Jews from the country would soon come to pass. Little did the king realize that in doing this, he had signed the death warrant for his own beloved Queen Esther.

Mordecai uncovered the plot to eliminate the Jews. The Bible says that Mordecai tore his clothes (a sign of mourning for either national or personal disaster) and put on sackcloth and ashes (more signs of mourning or for prayers of deliverance). This strange behavior of Mordecai ended up being reported back to Queen Esther. The Bible says, in Esther 4:4–7,

> When Esther's maids and eunuchs came and told her about Mordecai, she was in great distress. She sent clothes for him to put on instead of his sackcloth, but he would not accept them. Then Esther summoned Hathach, one of the king's eunuchs assigned to attend her, and ordered him to find out what was troubling Mordecai and why. So Hathach went out to Mordecai in the open square of the city in front of the king's gate. Mordecai told him everything that had happened to him, including the exact amount of money Haman had promised to pay into the royal treasury for the destruction of the Jews.

Mordecai told Hathach "to urge her to go into the king's presence to beg for mercy and plead with him for her people" (Esther 4:8).

Esther knew how difficult Mordecai's request would be. In preparation to become the queen, Esther had gone through a rigorous education of how to please the king, which included the strict rules and regulations of his court. The law in those days prohibited someone from just showing up in the king's presence without first being summoned. That applied even to the queen. If someone did show up in the presence of the king without having been summoned and it displeased the king, the action could result in a death sentence. The person could lose his or her life at the order of the king.

Mordecai received some pushback from Queen Esther, because she knew the law and that she could possibly lose her life. At this, Mordecai made this often-quoted statement, "And who knows but that you have come to royal position for such a time as this?" (Esther 4:14)

With that, Esther sent a message back to Mordecai: "Go, gather together all the Jews who are in Susa, and *fast* for me. Do not eat or drink for three days, night or day. I and my maids will *fast* as you do. When this is done, I will go to the king, even though it is against the law. And if I perish, I perish" (Esther 4:15, emphasis added).

Esther got it! She understood the dire straits they were facing. She also knew how to call upon the Almighty for deliverance. She obviously knew about the power of fasting. Matthew Henry, in his commentary, states, "Esther then decided, whatever it might cost her, to turn to the king, but not until she and her friends had first turned to God. With the godliness and devotion of an Israelite, for she believed that God's favor could be gained by prayer. She knew it was the practice of good people, in extraordinary cases, to add fasting to prayer."[27] The Bible is silent on this matter; however, she had probably been taught the power of fasting from a very early age, maybe even by Mordecai. She knew she would be risking her life. She also knew if something wasn't done, the Jews, along with herself, could all lose their lives.

The outcome of the story was that Haman's plot was revealed, and he was hung on the gallows that he had built for the hanging of Mordecai. The genocide was stopped! The Jews, to this day, celebrate this story through the Feast of Purim in thanksgiving to God and in remembrance for what Esther accomplished.

This three-day fast was another example of a fast to *stave off disaster*. It was not only a partnership fast; it was also a corporate fast. Esther knew what needed to happen. She knew the risks. She also knew that she needed divine intervention. It is interesting to read that Esther was the one calling for the fast and not Mordecai. Her cousin Mordecai, who had played a significant role in her life as her adopted father, should have been the one calling for the fast. Instead, it was Esther. She, as well as Mordecai, humbled themselves through this fast in order to implore their God on behalf of the people who were about to be exterminated.

King Jehoshaphat

King Jehoshaphat reigned around 873–849 BC. The story picks up in 2 Chronicles 20. We learn in earlier passages that King Jehoshaphat was a good king who, in his early years, had been fully devoted to the Lord. However, he was not without fault, as he had made three disastrous alliances during his rule. In 2 Chronicles 20, verses 1–3, his advisors told him that a vast army was coming against him and the nation. Verse 3 says, "Alarmed, Jehoshaphat resolved to inquire of the Lord, and he proclaimed a fast for all of Judah." I would like to focus on four words: alarmed, resolved, inquire, and fast.

ALARMED

King Jehoshaphat was rightfully alarmed. In this biblical narrative, counselors describe the army as vast. This would indicate that this invading army was prepared for war and that they would do anything to succeed in their military operation. *Webster's Dictionary Online* defines *alarm* as "sudden surprise with fear or terror excited by apprehension of danger; in the military use, commonly, sudden apprehension of being attacked by surprise." King Jehoshaphat was extremely disturbed because he knew that losing the battle would most likely result in the annihilation of himself, his family, and his people. Being alarmed is not necessarily a bad thing. It is a human emotion to see danger and try to avoid it. Proverbs 22:3 says, "A prudent man sees danger and takes refuge, but the simple keep going and suffer for it." King Jehoshaphat was a prudent man, so he took his struggle to the next level.

RESOLVE

King Jehoshaphat did not know what to do. In verse 12, the Bible says, "For we have no power to face this vast army that is attacking us. We do not know what to do, but our eyes are upon you." Impending doom was overtaking him. He might have even thought that his army could not defeat the vast, approaching army. The Bible says that he *resolved* to inquire of the Lord. *Resolve*, as defined by *Webster's Dictionary Online*, is "to determine or decide in purpose; to make ready in mind; to fix; to settle." This is exactly what King Jehoshaphat attempted to do. The threat of the invasion was more than he could figure out on his own. He didn't know what to do. He made a determination, a resolve, to *inquire* of the Lord.

INQUIRE

There is no end to the struggles of life. Being a pastor out and about in the community, I hear story after story of the daily trials that all believers go through, not to mention the life-and-death struggles faced by Christians all over the world. There is no shortage of believers who are going through incredible trials in their lives. Once again, I will restate my position that as Americans, we are very prosperous, and that prosperity has lulled us into a false sense of security. Our prosperity and education have trained us to figure out and solve problems on our own.

I hear very few believers say that they need to inquire of the Lord as to their next steps in figuring out a particular difficulty that they are facing. This is not good because at this point all we have are our feelings. Many times I hear believers say, "I am feeling led to (fill in the blank)."

When I hear statements like this, I wonder, "Being led by whom: God or Satan?" My former pastor, Bob Moorehead, once said, "Sin will take you places that you never wanted to go, keep you there longer than you ever wanted to stay, and cost you more than you ever wanted to pay." Over the years, I have tweaked that saying by replacing "sin" with "feelings": "Feelings will take you places that you never wanted to go, keep you there longer than you ever wanted to stay, and cost you more than you ever wanted to pay." So many times Christians embark down a path based on *feelings*. I know this has been the case many different times in my life.

That is why it is so very important to separate yourself from your feelings. Seek the Lord in prayer, and cover that with a season of fasting. This will enable you to hear from Him for the correct direction. I have seen too many businessmen impale themselves on the sword of feelings. They exercised what they thought was sound judgment, only to find the direction they went was not the direction the Lord had ordained for themselves or their families.

FAST

We always gloss over that one word, "fast." King Jehoshaphat did not know in the physical realm what to do to thwart this enemy. But he did know what to do in the spiritual realm. He said, in verse 12, "Our eyes are upon you."

King Jehoshaphat gathered the people of Judah to seek help from the Lord. The Bible says that Jehoshaphat stood up in the assembly of the people and prayed with fervor and sincerity. The last two verses of his prayer share his heart: "For we have no power to face this vast army that is attacking us. We do not know what to do, but our eyes are upon you" (2 Chronicles 20:12).

Again, we see the leader taking steps to inquire of the Lord. The leader readily admits that this trial is beyond him. The king and the people were in a terrifying situation. They were afraid of losing their families and their lives. There was nowhere to turn but to the Lord. Like the Israelites fleeing Pharaoh and coming to the banks of the Red Sea, they had no choice but to trust God for their protection. This is the exact place many believers find themselves today. This is also the exact spot where God does some of His finest works in our lives.

The story goes on to tell us that a prophet by the name of Jahaziel stood up in the assembly and spoke these words in verse 15: "Do not be afraid or discouraged because of this vast army. For the battle is not yours but God's...You will not have to fight this battle. Take up your positions; stand firm and see the deliverance the Lord will give you, O Judah and Jerusalem. Do not be afraid; do not be discouraged. Go out to face them tomorrow and the Lord will be with you."

When you fast with the right motives, there is something in the heavenlies that moves the hand of God. Time and time again we see examples of this. When you are knee-deep in your own personal trials, and you are standing at the shores of your own Red Sea—what are you going to do? Fast! What is your Red Sea? Is your marriage of twenty-five years falling apart? Fast! Have you been falsely accused of something at work? Fast! Has someone you know just been diagnosed with an inoperable tumor? Fast! Are you plagued with fear and anxiety over the future? Fast!

In the passage with King Jehoshaphat, God speaks through the prophet Jahaziel and tells the nation not to be afraid, that the battle is His. What an incredible promise! The Lord promised that He would fight their battle. He would be their rear guard.

Next, King Jehoshaphat does something most astounding, which has never been duplicated again in the Bible. He puts the men's choir in front of the army and instructs them to march out singing praise songs to the Lord. Huh? He did what? You heard me. King Jehoshaphat instructed the men's choir to march out in front of all the military men, who were carrying their weapons of war, and instructed them to start singing praises to God.

The vast army that was coming up against Judah was composed of three different armies. In the Bible it states that each of the armies started rising up against one another until they were all ultimately annihilated. King Jehoshaphat arrived at an overlook with the men's choir and the army only to see the valley strewn with dead bodies. The Bible says it took his crew three days to collect all of the plunder. They suffered no losses—no losses in gear and no losses in life. They didn't have to raise one arm against one adversary—they just showed up. When God tells us not to be afraid for He is going to fight our battles for us, He means it. How would you like to face a trial that ended with you collecting the plunder?

What would have been the outcome if King Jehoshaphat had not *resolved* to *inquire* of the Lord and call a *fast*? We read this story, and we become excited to see how the Lord delivered His people. But we gloss right over that one word...*fast*. He fasted. In the beginning he called a fast. Fasting with the right motives causes us to humble ourselves before the Lord. The problem with Americans is that we think we are very smart. We want to solve our problems immediately. We shoot up one or two prayers and think we have a clear direction from the Lord; on the contrary, we are only providing lip service to the discipline of prayer.

Towns once again states,

Periodically, political leaders have declared a national day of prayer and fasting for divine intervention in crisis situations. In 1588, the victory of Sir Francis Drake over the Spanish Armada was widely recognized by the English as an act of divine intervention.

The Pilgrims fasted the day before disembarking from the Mayflower in 1620, as they prepared to establish a mission colony to reach the native people of North America. It was common for political leaders in many New England villages to call for a fast when they faced a crisis.

Friday, February 6, 1756 was designated a day of solemn fasting and prayer in England over war with France in the Americas. Lincoln also called for a national day of prayer and fasting during the Civil War. On both occasions, military victories by England and the northern states of the United States were viewed as divine interventions by those who fasted and prayed for those successes.

Similar days of prayer and fasting have been proclaimed by political leaders as recently as World War II. In the midst of the Battle of Britain, George VI designated Sunday, September 8, 1940, as a day of prayer and fasting. In a radio broadcast made days after the day of prayer, British Prime Minister Winston Churchill compared Britain's state with the earlier threats of the Spanish Armada and Napoleon. In his memoirs, Churchill identified September 15 (the Sunday following the day of prayer) as "the crux of the Battle of Britain." After the war, it was learned that Hitler decided to postpone his planned invasion of Britain for two days (September 17). Similar calls for a day of prayer also accompanied the D-Day invasion of Europe by the allies on June 6, 1944.

In short, fasting has a long and impressive history as a discipline adopted by believers for a variety of reasons, but all of them are connected by the principle of self-denial. We may deny the self to emphasize the needs of the nation, or others who need God's blessing or of our own spiritual needs.[28]

Nevertheless, when exercised with a pure heart and a right motive, fasting may provide us with a key to unlock doors where other keys have failed; a window opening up new horizons in the unseen world; a spiritual weapon of God's providing, mighty, to the pulling down of strongholds.[29]

Arthur Wallis

§

CHAPTER 12

What Are the Overlooked Keys to Fasting?

IN ORDER TO fully grasp fasting, you must comprehend the three misunderstood and overlooked keys to fasting: Isaiah 58, humbleness, and the meaning of "afflicting one's soul."

Key One–Understanding the Importance of Isaiah 58

Understanding Isaiah 58 is of paramount importance in understanding the discipline of fasting. In this passage, God is speaking through His prophet Isaiah. In the first few verses, God admonishes the nation for their pathetic attempt at fasting. They were fasting, but they were complaining that they were not getting their way. They did not see anything changing in their personal struggles and trials. The Lord cut through their façade of false religion, showmanship, and unwillingness to change their sinful lives. Then, in His merciful way, He showed them what He expected of them in verses 6–7. He listed areas of weakness in their daily lives that needed to be cleaned up.

We undertook a more complete study on this matter in chapter 9. I would suggest the reader go back and read Isaiah 58 along with chapter 9 of this book. Then the Lord lists twelve incredible promises that He may bestow upon His children according to His will, if they will only fast with the right motives. Any one of these promises would change someone's life permanently. I desire that the Lord bestow these promises upon my family and me.

Key Two—Understanding the Importance of Humbleness

In order to gain a full understanding of the importance of humbleness, let's again take a look at Jonah. We know the story. Jonah ends up in Nineveh and preaches eight words; then the Ninevites turn from their evil ways and humble themselves before God. We have to ask ourselves, what did this pagan nation know about fasting? Even the king proclaimed a fast. After the king's call for a fast, the Bible says, "When God saw what they did and how they turned from their evil ways, he had compassion and did not bring upon them the destruction he had threatened" (Jonah 3:10). God turned from what He had planned to do to this evil nation for one reason: they humbled themselves through fasting. They backed that up by turning from their evil ways. To understand this passage, we must understand the spiritual link between humbleness and compassion. Humbleness has been evidenced in different biblical stories, causing God to stay his hand of judgment.

In 1 Kings 21 we are told another story about the evil King Ahab, who did much evil in the eyes of the Lord. The prophet Elijah had been instructed by the Lord to pronounce judgment on King Ahab. Upon hearing those words, the king promptly tore his clothes, put sackcloth on his body, fasted, lay in sackcloth, and went about mourning. This evil king, upon hearing of his coming destruction, fasted. He got it. He fasted and mourned. He humbled himself in the sight of a Holy God. The Bible says in verse 29, "Have you noticed how Ahab has humbled himself before me? Because he has humbled himself, I will not bring this disaster in his day." King Ahab's humbling of himself actually turned away God's hand of destruction.

Arthur Wallis, in his book *God's Chosen Fast*, states of King Ahab, "Judgment was deferred because even such a man as Ahab was prepared to humble his soul with fasting. How great is God's mercy! How great the power of fasting to call it forth!"[30]

Another story where the humbling of oneself moved the hand of God, is found in 2 Chronicles 33. This is the story of King Manasseh, also an evil king. The Bible says in verse 6 that "He [King Manasseh] did much evil in the eyes of the Lord, provoking Him to anger." God so loved King Manasseh and his people that He attempted to move their hearts and draw them back to Him, but they paid no attention. So the Lord brought the Assyrian army against Manasseh and the nation. As a result, Manasseh was taken as a prisoner.

As a king, Manasseh had it all. He had power, might, prestige, and material possessions. When he was taken prisoner, he lost it all. While he was in prison, he cried out to the Lord. The Bible says in verse 12, "In his distress he sought the favor of the Lord his God and humbled himself greatly before the God of his fathers." The outcome of this biblical story was that the Lord, moved by King Manasseh's sincere prayer and humbleness, restored him back to his kingdom in Jerusalem. Once again we see the power of humbleness moving the hand of God. Sometimes God relents from His prescribed judgment on an individual or a nation due to their genuine act of humbleness.

One of my favorite scriptures is 2 Chronicles 7:14. It reads, "If my people, who are called by my name, will humble themselves and pray and seek my face and turn from their wicked ways, then will I hear from heaven, and will forgive their sin and will heal their land." In this passage, there are four "ifs"—humble, pray, seek, and turn. These are all very important "ifs." Sometimes, to fully realize the meaning of any passage, we must seek the order in which things are listed. God is God and could have listed these items in any particular order, but He placed humble first.

There is a direct contrast to being humble of heart and being proud. The Bible speaks against the proud. But first, let's look toward the Bible to see what it has to say about humbleness.

Psalm 18:27—"You save the humble but bring low those whose eyes are haughty."

Psalm 25:9—"He guides the humble in what is right and teaches them his way."

Psalm 149:4—"For the Lord takes delight in his people, he crowns the humble with salvation."

Proverbs 3:34—"He mocks proud mockers but gives grace to the humble."

James 4:6—"God opposes the proud but gives grace to the humble."

In contrast, this is what the Bible says about proud people.

Psalm 31:23—"The Lord preserves the faithful, but the proud he pays back in full."

Psalm 101:5—"Whoever has haughty eyes and a proud heart, him will I not endure."

Psalm 138:6—"Though the Lord is on high, he looks upon the lowly, but the proud he knows from afar."

Proverbs 16:5—"The Lord detests all the proud of heart. Be sure of this: They will not go unpunished."

Proverbs 21:4—"Haughty eyes and a proud heart, the lamp of the wicked, are sin!"

Stuart Scott, in his book *From Pride to Humility*, states,

You cannot have humility where pride exists. Pride is the opposite of humility and it is one of the most loathed sins in God's sight. Pride is an epidemic vice. It is everywhere and manifests itself in many ways.[31]

When someone is proud he or she is focused on self...To sum it all up, proud people believe that life is all about *them*—their happiness, their accomplishments and their worth.[32]

Key Three—Understanding the Importance of Afflicting One's Soul

In Leviticus 16:29, the Lord outlines the requirements for the only day He commands His people to fast: the Day of Atonement or Yom Kippur. In that verse, He uses the words, "You shall afflict your souls" (NKJV). To some Bible scholars and commentators, afflicting one's soul means fasting. We must dig deeper to fully grasp the uniqueness of these five words. In some of the newer translations, afflicting your soul is translated into humbling your soul.

Every part of the body has been mapped. We can visualize what each part of the body looks like. If I went to a third grade class and asked them to draw a hand, they could do so. If I asked them to draw an eye, they could do so. If I went to an eighth grade class and asked the students to draw a heart—or a kidney or a tongue—they could do so. However, if I asked them to draw a soul, they would have a difficult time, just as you or I would have. We believe the soul exists because the Bible tells us it does. We believe that when we die, the soul lives on, and we will be given glorified bodies. When we fast and go without food or drink, our bodies are afflicted. But what does it mean to afflict one's soul?

The Hebrew person understood the connection between our bodies needing food for nourishment and how that compared to the eternal soul. On the website New-Life.net, in an article called "Biblical Fasting: What It Is and How to Do It," the author writes,

> We gain some insight here about how the Hebrews viewed fasting. Fasting is more than just "afflicting one's body." It is "afflicting one's *soul*." In other words, fasting in the Hebrew mind is something my soul participates in. Fasting is denying myself. It is denying not only my own body, but also my own wants. It is a way of saying that food and my desires are secondary to something else. Fasting is afflicting one's soul—an act of self-denial… Because Biblical fasting always occurs together with prayer in the Bible—ALWAYS. You can pray without fasting, but you cannot

fast (Biblically speaking) without praying. Biblical fasting is deliberately abstaining from food for a spiritual reason: communication and relationship with the Father.[33]

One of the greatest spiritual benefits of fasting is becoming more attentive to God.[34]

Elmer L. Towns

CHAPTER 13

More on Fasting

IF YOU FAST one day a week, don't expect to have many adverse reactions except hunger pains, some slight dizziness, and maybe some headaches from caffeine withdrawal. If you ever do feel that something is adversely occurring in your body, you should contact your medical practitioner immediately. If you decide to fast for extended periods of time, you can expect your body to scream at you. If you are a coffee or soda drinker, your body may have acclimated to caffeine and sugar, and maybe experiencing withdrawal symptoms.

I suggest you stop drinking caffeinated products during your fasts. If you do this, the body likely will respond with headaches. These headaches should subside after a couple of days. In addition, you may experience dizziness due to blood sugar swings. You will also experience diarrhea. Over time, this too should subside. On extended fasts, you will always want to make sure your spouse is aware of your fasting—especially if he or she is doing the cooking. Also, it is a must that you inform your medical practitioner before you begin fasting.

Who Should Never Fast?

Please understand that fasting for any length of time can be harmful to your body. Fasting is not for everyone. The rule of thumb is, always consult with your physician before undertaking a fast, and know your body! Use godly discernment to determine if God is calling you to either a short-term or a longer-term fast. Consult with your spouse, your pastor, your accountability partners, and especially your physician about your desires to fast. This book was written solely from a spiritual perspective and is based on my personal fasting experience.

I am not a medical doctor; however, I have attempted to compile a list (below) of people who should never fast. This is *not* an *exhaustive* list. If you choose to go forward with a spiritual fast, you should have your own physical condition assessed by your medical practitioner before embarking on that journey. Once into a fast, if your body is telling you something, seek immediate medical assistance.

1. *Life-threatening diseases*. Anyone with diabetes (type 1 or 2), anyone who is currently undergoing chemo or radiation treatments, anyone who has heart-related issues or cancer issues, or anyone who is currently preparing for or recovering from surgery—these people should not fast.

2. *Pregnant or nursing mothers*. Pregnant and nursing moms should never fast as this could potentially rob the mother and baby of much-needed nutrients. Maintaining a healthy, balanced diet is most important for pregnant and nursing mothers.

3. *Children*. Children should never be encouraged to fast as this could possibly rob them of necessary nutrients during growth spurts. Children could be encouraged to fast from dessert, TV, video games, or texting.

4. *Compromised immune systems*. Those suffering from comprised immune systems or autoimmune disorders also should not fast as this could be a further detriment to their health.

5. *Mental health issues*. Any individuals suffering from any type of mental health issues should never be encouraged to fast as this could cause further swings in mood and temperament.

6. *Eating disorders*. Fasting could be a temptation for individuals with eating disorders to indulge in an unbiblical diet, or it could cause them to become addicted to fasting. Spiritual fasting should never be confused with diet or a weight-loss programs.

Those Who Should Be Cautioned When Considering Fasting

In addition to the list above, there is a sublist of those who should be highly cautioned when considering fasting.

1. *Elderly.* The elderly, because of the potential of compromised immune systems, are oftentimes quite susceptible to disease. The elderly should be cautioned and should definitely seek medical advice before embarking on a spiritual fast of any length of time.

2. *Prescription drug usage.* If you are taking any prescription drugs, you must consult with your physician as to how your fasting might interact with your medications. We live in a new age of complex prescriptions drugs. Some medications require an empty stomach, while others require food in your stomach. Those who are fasting must know their bodies, the prescription drugs they are taking, and how a lack of solid food will affect their physical well-being while on medications. When in doubt, consult your physician.

3. *Exertion.* Individuals who exert their bodies every day in the course of making a living (such as construction workers or athletes) do need to be aware of the body's reaction to having no food. Athletes who rigorously exercise every day should seriously consider forgoing strenuous workouts while fasting. Fasting and strenuous workouts can't coexist. Do one or the other; don't do both.

Those who fall within this list of people who are cautioned against fasting may want to consider the Daniel Fast, which I will address later in this chapter. As mentioned several times, neither of these lists is meant to be exhaustive. The key to fasting is *prayerful confirmation* to go forward with your fast, and above all, *know your body!* Fasting can be dangerous to your health if done improperly and with the wrong motives.

What Fasting Is Not?

In order to understand what fasting is, we first must understand what fasting is not. Pastor Steve Walker of Canyon Hills Community Church, in his sermon on fasting, succinctly puts it, "Fasting is not one of the rituals, gimmicks, or tricks that we do to get God to do what we want Him to do."[35] I have outlined four items below to consider before embarking on your first fast:

1. ***Fasting is not a religious ritual.*** Jesus always corrected bad fasting or fasting for show. He spoke against the Pharisees multiple times, admonishing them for their improper way of fasting. Jesus hates hypocritical fasting. We have learned about Jesus's teachings in a previous chapter.

2. ***Fasting is not a genie in the bottle.*** Fasting is not meant to be a manipulative tool to get God's attention on how holy or righteous you are. Fasting does not guarantee your prayers will be answered. It is not a method to twist God's arm in an attempt to win His approval for answered prayer.

3. ***Fasting has never been meant for showmanship.*** The Old Testament speaks about the wrong kinds of fasting in Isaiah chapter 58, which was discussed in chapter 9. Jesus also spoke against the Pharisees' showmanship in the Bible, which was discussed in chapter 10.

4. ***Fasting is never a weight-loss philosophy.*** For those who have struggled with weight issues all their lives, they need to understand that fasting as a weight-loss program is never encouraged or promoted in the Bible. People who have struggled with weight issues or eating disorders should be strongly cautioned against becoming addicted to fasting for purposes of losing weight. People who have struggled with bulimia or anorexia should consult with both their medical practitioners and their mental health specialists before undertaking a fast.

What Is the Daniel Fast?

There are two different examples in the book of Daniel where Daniel *adjusted* his eating. Both are referenced today in the mainstream of society as the Daniel Fast. The first example is found in Daniel 1:8–16. This particular situation requires the abstaining from a specific kind of food, such as meat. For this fast, Daniel asked his handler, the king's chief official in charge of the new recruits that he and his friends be allowed to abstain from some of the king's food. In verse 8, the Bible reads, "But Daniel resolved not to defile himself with the royal food and wine, and he asked the chief official for permission not to defile himself this way."

This one verse gives us a snapshot into the heart of Daniel. He knew he was in a foreign land being assimilated into the culture. For Daniel, this was a matter of conscience for two reasons. First, he was raised to understand Jewish law. To eat certain foods would violate the Mosaic law in Leviticus 11. Secondly, this meat was most likely dedicated to the idols of Babylon. Eating it would be in direct contradiction to the law and would be acknowledging their idols as deities. This particular withdrawal from certain types of food lasted ten days. In Daniel 1:15–16, we see the outcome. "At the end of the ten days they looked healthier and better nourished than any of the young men who ate the royal food. So the guard took away their choice food and the wine they were to drink and gave them vegetables instead."

Many today confuse and misinterpret this dietary request found in chapter 1 to be the Daniel Fast. It is not. In order for a fast to be a fast, there needs to be some spiritual component. This most likely was a lifestyle change that continued until Daniel was out of training in the king's court. Don't get me wrong, I am a strong proponent of taking care of the temple. I know how easy it is to gain weight and how hard it is to lose it. It is all about the real motivations of the heart. The point is, if you need to lose weight, and you're using this ten-day example given in Daniel chapter 1 as a model, then call it what it is—a weight-loss program and not a spiritual fast.

The second example of the Daniel Fast is found in chapter 10 and would be considered the true Daniel Fast. Before this particular fast, Daniel was given a revelation. The revelation was so concerning to Daniel that the Bible says, "At that time I, Daniel, mourned for three weeks. I ate no choice food; no meat or wine touched my lips; and I used no lotions at all until the three weeks were over" (Daniel 10:2–3). This fast lasted twenty-one days and eliminated choice foods much like when he was in the king's court. However, his motive behind eliminating certain foods was due to a deep mourning of the soul. Daniel was deeply troubled by this dream and therefore sought the Almighty in this time of need.

The Daniel Fast truly seems to be in vogue in America right now. The Internet is awash in information concerning the Daniel Fast. After scanning a number of websites, it is my fear that people are using this fast to lose weight and not for the spiritual component. Any purpose for fasting other than for spiritual reasons is repulsive and offensive to God, as outlined in Isaiah 58 and in Jesus's admonishment of the Pharisees in the New Testament. Some may ask, what about when my doctor tells me I need to fast overnight for a blood draw or medical procedure. Is that repulsive to God? Of course not, the key is that you are not fasting for a spiritual fast.

I believe that there are many Christians struggling in America because of their weight and the excessive amount of food that we have at our fingertips. Some on the Internet might use the Daniel Fast as described in Daniel chapter 1 to sell a book or product for weight loss. Buyer beware!

Having said that, I do believe the Daniel Fast (as described in chapter 10) has a great deal of merit for those who cannot abstain from solid food but truly desire to enter into a season of fasting in order to draw closer to God. There are people who, because of their biological makeup, cannot abstain from solid foods. This would include anyone that would fall into the list as outlined under *Who Should Never Fast*, or *Those Who Should Be Cautioned When Considering Fasting*. Be careful, always consult with your physician before undertaking a fast, and know your body.

Sidebar

I had a great opportunity to sit with other believers and watch an awesome video series on the book of Daniel. We finally arrived at Daniel chapter 10. I knew what was coming and waited with great anticipation to hear if there would be anything said on the Daniel Fast in verse 3. Nothing! Nada! Zippo! I do understand—completely. I get it. There is only so much time for the video lecture. The objectives and priorities were different, not focused on fasting. What was expounded upon was incredibly insightful wisdom into chapter 10 and was of great value to those of us listening in our group.

However, there were two incredible *links* that were missed or glossed over that I think will drive home the point of the importance of fasting. In Daniel 10:3, the prophet says he fasted for three weeks, or twenty-one days. Then in verses 12–13 the Bible says, "Do not be afraid, Daniel. Since the first day that you set your mind to *gain understanding* and to *humble* yourself before your God, your words were heard, and I have come in response to them. But the prince of the Persian kingdom resisted me *twenty-one* days. Then Michael, one of the chief princes, came to help me, because I was detained there with the king of Persia" (emphasis added).

Link One

In chapter 12 of this book, I list three keys that anyone who is undertaking the discipline of fasting must grasp. Let's review those three keys.

Key One—Understanding the Importance of Isaiah 58
Key Two—Understanding the Importance of Humbleness
Key Three—Understanding the Importance of Afflicting One's Soul

It must be stated and restated that there is a direct connection between humbling oneself and fasting. In Daniel 10:12, the angel says, "Since the first day that you set your mind to *gain understanding* and to *humble* yourself before your God, *your words were heard,* and I have come in response

124

to them" (emphasis added). So what was the first day? It was the first day of his fast.

In Isaiah 58:9, the Bible says, "Then you will call, and the Lord will answer." This is Promise Five that I list in chapter 9 of this book. Believer, there is a direct correlation between humbling oneself in fasting and the promises listed in Isaiah 58.

LINK TWO

The Bible says that Daniel fasted for twenty-one days. It also says the angel was "delayed" for twenty-one days and then showed up. What is the link? Can the two twenty-one days be interrelated? Unfortunately, the Bible is silent on the matter. Where the Bible is silent, I will *not* attempt to create new teachings, dogmas, or doctrines. However, I have freedom in Christ to at least ask the questions—what could possibly be the link? Or is there even a link between the two spans of twenty-one days mentioned in verses 3 and 13?

I don't believe we can fully grasp the importance of this passage on this side of eternity. In chapter 18 of this book, I speak of the rocket launcher. Without ruining the ending to the book by going into too much detail, I compare prayer to the soldier's rifle and fasting to the soldier's rocket launcher. I (and others who fast regularly) believe fasting opens the gates of heaven. I believe there is an unimaginable spiritual battle taking place in the heavenlies for the souls of men. I believe fasting is a grossly misunderstood spiritual discipline being looked down upon by some in the church as a practice only religious fanatics follow. Don't be duped! Beloved, this is a spiritual tool given to us by the Almighty to equip us for the spiritual fight. The question is—will you pick up this spiritual tool and engage the enemy?

What Are the Steps to Starting a Fast?

Some people struggle with how to even begin a fast. Starting a lifelong habit of fasting, like any other habit you wish to develop, takes discipline.

125

It's not complicated, but it does take resolve and fortitude. Below are ten steps to assist you in this next step of your spiritual journey. If you resolve to follow these steps, the fasting that seems unnatural now will soon become a natural part of your Christian walk.

Step One—*Be prayed up.* Ask the Lord for direction as you start your new lifelong discipline of fasting. Seek His face and His will for your life. Ask the Holy Spirit to direct your steps and to give you strength.

Step Two—*Reread Isaiah 58.* This is a key passage to understand as you embark on this new way of life. Reread verses 3 and 4 for the reasons why God was not answering the cry of those who were fasting. Then reread verses 6 and 7 and meditate on what the Lord is asking of you when you fast. It is important, as you read these verses, to ask the Lord to reveal to you any areas of your life that need to be strengthened, corrected, or confessed, as well as any relationships that need to be restored. Read with *inquisitive* passion verses 8–11. Meditate on these promises. I suggest that you write out the twelve promises on paper and keep it somewhere to review. You could put them on your computer or smartphone. You might print them out in larger letters and post them on your bathroom mirror or refrigerator. Do you desire any of these promises? If yes, then you should fast.

Step Three—*Complete the six Bible study lessons on fasting in the appendix of this book.* It is always prudent to further your knowledge of God's principles by digging deeper into His Word. Study by yourself, with a friend, or in your Bible-study group. Whatever you do, dig deeper. The general topic of these studies is Isaiah 58, Pride vs. Humbleness, the Nineveh Fast, the Esther Fast, King Jehoshaphat's Fast, and the Ezra Fast.

Step Four—*Consult your physician.* Please understand that fasting for any length of time can be harmful to your body. Fasting is not for everyone. The rule of thumb is to always consult with your physician before undertaking a fast, and know your body! Review the section on *Who Should Never Fast*, and *Those Who Should Be Cautioned When Considering Fasting*.

Step Five—*Start out slowly.* Pick a target day next week. Pick a day when you have no lunch or dinner appointments scheduled. Start small. Commit to fast one or two meals that day—maybe fast for breakfast and lunch, and have your evening meal as planned. Then in the following weeks, commit to fasting for three consecutive meals. Foster sums it up even better:

> As with all the disciplines, a progression should be observed; it is wise to learn to walk well before we try to run. Begin with a partial fast of twenty-four-hours' duration; many have found lunch to lunch to be the best time. This means that you would not eat two meals. Fresh fruit juices are excellent to drink during the fast. Attempt this once a week for several weeks. In the beginning you will be fascinated with the physical aspects of your experience, but the most important thing to monitor is the inner attitude of the heart. Outwardly you will be performing the regular duties of your day, but inwardly you will be in prayer and adoration, song, and worship. In a new way, cause every task of the day to be a sacred ministry to the Lord. However mundane your duties, for you they are a sacrament. Break your fast with a light meal of fresh fruits and vegetables and a good deal of inner rejoicing. After having achieved several fasts with a degree of spiritual success, move on to a thirty-six-hour fast: three meals. With that accomplished, it is time to seek the Lord as to whether He wants you to go on a longer fast. Three to seven days is a good time period and will probably have a substantial impact on the course of your life.[36]

Step Six—*Communicate.* Talk to God, talk to your spouse, talk to your doctor, and talk to your family on what the Lord is leading you to do. Explain the process you went through to arrive at this point of stepping out in faith to undertake this fast. Share with them the promises of Isaiah

58 and the specific prayer requests that you are lifting up in your daily fasts. Open up your heart as you share your passion for a fresh touch from God.

Step Seven—*Go to the grocery store.* Go to the store and buy a jug or two of your favorite juice. Experiment! There is nothing worse than being mentally prepared for your fast and then having some juice that doesn't appeal to your sense of taste. Remember, many store-bought juices are full of sugar.

Step Eight—*Go to the office-supply store.* Buy a nice leather binder to keep a journal. It doesn't have to be very expensive, but find something that isn't flimsy and won't become warped over time. It needs to last a lifetime. It will become a keepsake for you in the years to come.

Step Nine—*List out three prayer requests.* It is imperative that you start out right. You must have right and pure motives. There must be a reason to fast. Whatever is burdening you should be listed as an item of prayer and fasting. In the beginning fasts, I would caution you to only have three or four specific prayers as your focus for the fast. If you happen to be an overachiever, you may be tempted to list thirty different prayer requests. I suspect there is nothing wrong with that; however, in the beginning you should only have a handful of requests that you can zero in on with laser-like precision.

Step Ten—*Commit.* Commit to fast one day a week for the next three months. Be purposeful and driven in committing to this goal.

How Should You Begin and End a Fast?

In answer to that question, I have one word—slowly! During a one-day fast, you should not see any real physical changes. However, anything longer than a three-day fast is going to cause your body to rebel. Before an extended fast, you should not be gorging yourself on heavy food. Stay away from foods that you like that could trigger cravings and be your downfall. Start out easy. Several days before your fast, start eating lighter foods, such as soups and broth.

Extra-special care should be taken when you come off of an extended fast. You heard me say that when I came off my fasts, I had a couple of bites of meatloaf and mashed potatoes. There is a cliché that states, "Don't do as I do, do as I say!" Well, I'm telling you: *Don't* have meatloaf and mashed potatoes! Start back into your eating routine with light foods such as soups, broth, and yogurt. Gradually, over a period of days and weeks, add back foods from your normal diet.

Does It Matter If We Fast?

Fasting is one of the most powerful tools that God has given us for our daily lives. In previous chapters of the book, I discussed what the Bible says about fasting. I referenced Isaiah 58 and Jesus's discourse on fasting.

Does it matter if we fast? Of course it does! What about you? What are you struggling with today? Do you need a fresh wind, a fresh fire to sweep your innermost being, as Pastor Jim Cymbala of the Brooklyn Tabernacle once said? Are you in need of a tender touch from God, or is there something in your life that is plaguing you that you know is not right? Are you in bondage to sin? Has the hand of addiction got its firm grasp around your neck in a death grip, or does it have its talons knee-deep in your brain and thought life? Maybe it is something as simple as being bored with your station in life. Maybe you are wandering fruitlessly in the dry desert of your soul, wondering where God is in your life. Or maybe you are single—desperately lonely and asking God why.

Pastor Steve Walker also says in his sermon on fasting, "Fasting confirms our utter dependence on God by finding in Him a strength beyond food because we are so desperate to satisfy our spiritual hunger. When we fast we want to be completely focused on Him, we trust God to meet our needs."[37]

The purpose of fasting is to take our eyes off of the material needs of this life and to focus purely on developing a closer, fully obedient, intimate walk with the Lord. Fasting brings us into a closer union with God. Floyd also writes,

Today, I write these words freely to demonstrate that my response comes from experience and deep personal conviction—my own personal pilgrimage—and is not motivated by a need to intellectualize the practice of fasting. Instead, as the sightless man whose only response to Jesus was, "Once I was blind, but now I see," so I, too, can say I have been changed inside and out. *I am not the same man, the same preacher, the same husband, or the same father I once was.* Fasting and prayer have been a <u>gateway</u> through which God has done supernatural things in my life, my family's life, and in my ministry. I have resolved that I *will never* face another *major decision* without first seeking the Lord's will and purpose through fasting and prayer. I am now also more convinced than ever that this miraculous *gateway* to God's supernatural intervention in the life of the believers is not exclusively reserved for a select few. It is the power of God available to everyone who trusts Jesus.[38] (Emphasis added.)

The self-denial and freedom of fasting and prayer provide a gateway for the supernatural power of God to come into our lives and minds, advancing the process of true freedom in Christ. After having completed short fasts and forty-day fasts, I honestly feel this enormous, almost *indescribable* freedom cannot be fully grasped in any other way. It is fervent prayer and fasting that reaches into the heart of God, *motivates* us to adjust to what God is doing, moves heaven into action, and changes what we see and do on earth.[39] (Emphasis added.)

Much like Dr. Floyd expresses above, I too can say that I am not the same husband, same preacher, same father, same boss, or same friend that I was before I learned the power of fasting. Fasting has changed me from the inside out. Fasting has changed me from living an uneventful, mediocre, and mundane Christian life to living one filled with purpose and wonderment. My Christian walk would have never known this added dimension had I not embraced the discipline of fasting. It is truly a gift from God, and I am so grateful to the Holy Spirit for teaching me. My hope is that the Christian reader who is wandering in a spiritual desert will experience a God-breathed, prayer-life revival and a new level of intimacy with the Lord.

Is There Ever an Occasion to End a Fast Prematurely?

I have already made mention of one time when a fast was broken. That first instance was when my wife and I were on a forty-day fast together while taking a trip to Florida for my aunt's eightieth birthday. You may recall that on a hot and extremely humid day, my wife passed out in a store. It was time for her to end her fast. When the body gives out, it is time for the fast to end. You must listen to your body when you fast!

An instance when *I* broke a fast happened when I had plans to take my new farmer friend out for lunch. I had planned not to eat at the restaurant. This is something I had done from time to time in the past when my fasting schedule and my personal schedule were on a collision course. It isn't an ideal situation because it makes people uncomfortable when they are eating and you are abstaining—but I make it work for me when the need arises.

After I arrived to pick up my friend to go to the restaurant, I found out that his eighty-year-old mother had cooked us a farm lunch. The rest of the family was also there, and I was considered a special guest. As I walked into the house, I asked the Lord what I should do. He said, "Eat what is placed in front of you." I had a situation; I inquired of the Lord and was at peace with His instructions to eat whatever was placed in front of me.

There is a third reason I have observed for breaking a fast. I have come across a number of people who have had a target goal of fasting for a specific period of time, only to end the fast early. When asked why they did not stay with their original plans, the response has always been, "The Lord told me to stop. It was complete."

The fact that I have observed this more than once from different people leads me to believe that the Spirit of the Lord does instruct some people to shorten their fasts. I am not one to question what someone hears from the Lord unless it is in direct conflict with sound, biblical teaching. However, the caution here is for the person who is fasting to be sure he or she is not listening to the wrong voice. The Bible says in 2 Corinthians 11:14, "And no wonder, for Satan himself masquerades as an angel of light." The person fasting needs to exercise extreme caution and discernment if he or she is being told to end a fast. One must be very certain that the voice is that of the Lord and not of the enemy.

I am reminded of the man of God from Judah in 1 Kings 13:8–25, who was instructed by the Lord not to eat or drink or go back the way he came. However, an older prophet came to him and said that the Lord had told him something different—that he was now to come back to *his* home to eat and drink. The man of God from Judah did so, but when he left the home of the older prophet, a lion came out and killed him. The Bible says that the older prophet lied to the man of God from Judah. Some theologians speculate that the man of God from Judah was killed by the lion because of his disobedience to God's instructions. He listened to someone who gave him advice contrary to what the Lord had instructed. We have an adversary who is a liar. He will whisper things to you that are contrary to God's instructions. Whatever you do, when considering breaking a fast, make sure you are listening to the right voice.

Another key is to understand that fasting cannot be seen as a legalistic form of spirituality. If there is anxiety or guilt over not completing a fast, one would need to double-check the motives for fasting. If you stop because you are succumbing to hunger pains or succumbing to family pressures, those reasons would be acts of disobedience—much like the man of God from Judah from the above example.

To review, there are three situations when a fast could legitimately come to an end before the target goal: (1) health reasons, (2) special situations, and (3) the Holy Spirit instructs you to stop.

Does the Bible Ever Speak of a Joyous Fast?

For several years we ran a discipleship house for men coming out of prison. Daren, one of the men who stayed there, once asked me if there was ever a time for a joyful fast. Without knowing it, he had stumped me. I had to stop in my tracks and think. No one had ever asked me that question before. I went on a superficial search and found nothing on joyful fasting. However, several years later in my normal Bible reading, I came across an obscure verse in Zechariah 8:19 that absolutely leaped off the page at me. "This is what the Lord Almighty says: 'The fasts of the fourth, fifth, seventh and tenth months will become joyful and glad occasions and happy festivals for Judah. Therefore love truth and peace.'" At first blush, I was elated. However, one must be very careful in taking one scripture alone and out of context.

Zechariah is one of the minor prophets. The book in its totality is written to the Jews in Jerusalem after they had returned from captivity in Babylon; its purpose was to give them a hope of deliverance through their blessed Messiah. They were a small remnant who had returned to rebuild the temple and their nation. The book of Zechariah is not only a book of prophetic messages about their Messiah's first coming, but it also foreshadows Christ's second coming and His millennial reign.

So the verse I had found (Zechariah 8:19) is all about the millennial kingdom when Christ will reign for a thousand years. There will be a time when fasting for sin, mourning over death, and answers to problems will not be needed. Those times will be *replaced* with "glad occasions and happy festivals" (Zechariah 8:19.) The NKJV says, "Shall be joy and gladness and cheerful feasts." This closely resembles Jesus's teaching in Matthew 9:14–15, when John's disciples confronted Jesus on why His disciples did not fast. So, we wait for our blessed Redeemer to return and *replace* our solemn fasts into times of feasts and festivals.

Fasting Is Not for Me!

Life never seems to have any shortage of trials. You don't have to look too far into your world—your friends, family, Bible study group, or business associates—to soon become overwhelmed with other people's problems. Life is difficult, and they are becoming more so as the last days become darker and darker. We need to train Christian warriors to use all the spiritual tools that God has given to His remnant to fight the good and faithful fight. When I go out to lunch with people, I hear many heartbreaking stories of true struggles and painful ordeals that individuals are facing.

It pains me to hear these stories. In the beginning, as I was learning the power of fasting, I was very shy in sharing about my fasting experiences. I am no longer shy, and I no longer care what people think of me when I bring up fasting. After a friend or an acquaintance has been totally transparent and left everything on the table in sharing the facts of a particular trial, I am able to offer some words of encouragement. I always ask, "Have you ever considered fasting for this situation?"

The responses I have received could fill a separate book. I have heard painfully honest responses like, "I am so deeply and spiritually spent, I can't even open my Bible, let alone think about fasting." When someone says that to me, I know the soul-pain is very deep. The situation that person is in really hurts. Some people confess, "I have never fasted and don't even know how to begin." And there are some who simply tune me out and quickly switch topics. I do understand that response. That would have been me. Had I not had my own personal experiences with fasting, I would have done the same thing—changed the subject!

The responses I don't understand are those such as "I am not called to fast" or "Fasting may be good for you, but I can't do it." But the best one yet is "No, fasting is not for me." I want to reach across the table and throttle some people. In essence, they are saying they would rather wallow in their pain and misery than give up a couple of meals to humble themselves before a holy and righteous God. My heart breaks for them. Little do they know what they are missing.

Floyd states, "If you have a fasting phobia, it's important that you begin by confessing and repenting of your fear. God will hear your prayer and will prepare your heart to respond specifically to His call. *Be willing to fast as the Holy Spirit directs.*"[40]

Closing Comments

I would be remiss if I did not touch upon the sovereignty of God in trials. What happens when you have fasted with pure motives and with the right agenda but the outcome is different than expected? When you have done everything right, but things did not turn out the way you had prayed? I fear that some who read this book will interpret fasting as a formula to attempt to get what they want from God. When things don't turn out their way, they will become angry at God. In a prior section, I listed four things that fasting is not. One of those four items was that fasting is not a form of a genie in a bottle or an attempt to twist God's arm.

The fact of the matter is, life is full of trials and difficulties. Bad things do happen. Loved ones do die before their time. Children do go astray. Cancer does kill. Teenage daughters do become pregnant. Car accidents do maim and destroy.

I was riding in the car the other day listening to a song by Lauren Daigle. I believe the lyrics of her song "Trust In You" sum up how we are to react when bad things happen to good people,

When you don't move the mountains
I'm needing you to move
When you don't part the waters
I wish I could walk through

When you don't give the answers
As I cry out to you
I will trust, I will trust, I will trust in you[41]

That sums it up. When we face trials of many kinds, no matter the outcome, we must trust in God. However, when walking through trials, remember a few things:

1. *God is God, and He alone is sovereign.* Some people who walk through trials become angry at God and walk away from Him when things don't go their way. They act out like spoiled little children. God is God, and we do not know His ways. He sees the big picture, especially the picture of the future plans He has for us. He is a loving God, even in the worst of trials. He loves you and promises never to leave you or forsake you. Hold on to those promises! When trials do not go your way, remember: seek him fervently, and He will be found.

2. *God's timing is not our timing.* There is a saying in Christendom that goes something like this: "God is never late, but seldom early." I don't like that saying! I believe that statement trivializes God and sets us up for discouragement when things don't turn out the way we had anticipated. We need to be careful about not putting God in a box, expecting to hear from Him in the eleventh hour. What happens when the eleventh hour passes? For many it does. The passing of the eleventh hour is perfect timing for the enemy to seek out and destroy through his tools of discouragement and anger. God does not operate in our time dimension.

3. *We do have a loving God.* God does love us. He loves us so much that He disciplines us when needed. He even allows us to go through gut-wrenching trials to mature us.

4. *Trials shape us for the future.* I am not the man I was twenty years ago for two reasons. First, I have grown in my love for and faith in

God. Second, the trials that I have walked through grew me and matured me.

5. ***Trials prepare us for ministry.*** There have been many instances in my past life when I did not have empathy for people who were going through specific trials. I couldn't relate to their particular trials. I often thought to myself, if they had done this or that, they wouldn't be in this painful situation. I often trivialized their problems with a statement like "All you need to do is..." Then I would fill in the blank with whatever obvious thing I thought they needed to do. Trials, however, are never that easy, and you cannot truly understand until you have walked through them yourself. Many times God allows us to walk through trials in order to shape us for those who come behind us with similar life struggles—in essence, preparation for future ministry.

6. ***Trials are meant to bring glory to God.*** How we act when we are walking through trials will either bring glory to God or dishonor to Him. I look back at my past life, the trials and struggles I was allowed to walk through, and I think of all the horrible reactions I had. I hang my head in shame. Thankfully, that is my past, not my future. The past is my Egypt; it is part of my patchwork quilt of life. It is where I came from, but not where I stayed. Though it will always be sown into my life quilt, I need not dwell in my past. My past reactions can also serve to produce a humbleness of heart going forward. "Oh Lord, let me have a do-over; let me not react that way again!" I will not allow my past to define my future. Trials are meant to bring glory to God. No matter how ugly your past might look, determine that your go-forward plan is to rely on Jesus the next time.

7. ***The Lord has said, "Never will I leave you; never will I forsake you"*** **(Hebrews 13:5).** What an incredible promise. This one verse in the Bible has brought me so much peace in my life. It should bring you peace as well.

Staving Off Disaster

I am not the same man, the same preacher, the same husband, or the same father I once was. Fasting and prayer have been a gateway through which God has done supernatural things in my life, my family's life, and in my ministry.[42]

Ronnie W. Floyd

§

CHAPTER 14

You Must Fast This Year

AT THE BEGINNING of 2007, it had been two years since my last extended fast. Once again, I felt the tugging of the Holy Spirit to start and complete another forty-day fast. At that time, Prisoners For Christ was extremely busy, with many aspects of the ministry expanding. One of the areas that was rapidly growing was the international outreach as we were developing field offices in different countries around the world. In the previous year, 2006, PFC had seen over 502,000 inmates in attendance at our PFC-sponsored church services and Bible studies around the world, with over 34,000 souls putting their trust in Jesus for the very first time. We had ministry work going full-bore on the home front, as well as the expansion we were experiencing on the international side. We had planned five overseas, short-term mission trips for 2007, and I was scheduled to be on four of those trips. Life was extremely busy.

One of the strategic priorities of the ministry was to open up an aftercare facility where drug addicts and alcoholics coming out of jail or prison could go to rebuild their lives and to draw close to the Lord. This was a twelve-year vision that culminated in the purchase of a forty-acre orchard in the middle of *nowheresville*, in the Lower Yakima Valley of Eastern Washington.

Over the years, the leadership of the ministry had considered many different pieces of property for this aftercare vision. It was a passion of many of our hearts. Having a Christ-centered aftercare facility was something truly lacking in the Pacific Northwest. We had come close to purchasing seven different pieces of property, only to have the doors slammed shut! After the last property slipped through our fingers, I threw up my hands and said, "Enough is enough; I am done!" I felt that the Lord had closed all the doors, and I was more than happy to move on.

It was at a Christmas party in 2005 that I was introduced to a farmer who had a piece of property for sale in Eastern Washington. He was very enthusiastic about the property and the potential of selling it for the work of a ministry. He seemed to think that his property might be the right location for our aftercare vision. He displayed a genuine interest in using his orchard for God's purposes. I had gently, but firmly, told him three different times at the party that, in no uncertain terms, I was no longer interested in looking for property for the aftercare vision. He was persistent.

He invited Rhonda and me to drive over and just take a look. Going and taking a look at this property felt like going and taking a look at a room full of puppies, where if you aren't careful, you will end up taking one home. Indeed, the property was just as he had described: out in the middle of nowhere, with virtually no neighbors, and quite beautiful to the eyes and soul. The property was just as I had envisioned our aftercare location would be—peaceful, calming to the soul, and a place for the lost and weary to find God.

There is just something special about country living. It is good for the soul. This country oasis seemed the perfect place for the broken to come to refresh their souls. I made no promises to my new farmer friend. I had shared with him the struggles of moving our former potential properties through the permitting process at the different county levels. However, I did say I would take one open door at a time. Sure enough, one open door led to another open door, which led to another open door, which ultimately led to our public hearing. Not one neighbor attended or protested our coming into their region of the Lower Yakima Valley with a clean-and-sober home. The gavel came down, and cheers went up. We were elated! We had never before succeeded this far in the permitting process. We were on our way to gaining the property we had so long sought.

Despite the initial victory, a strange thing happened to me as we rode the elevator down from our public hearing. I heard a still, small voice that said, "Don't do the deal!" Huh? Where did that come from? What was that all about? I filed it away and proceeded to keep it to myself. We were all ecstatic. I did not fast, nor did I inquire of the Lord to determine if this was the right direction for us to proceed. We had ten men and women on the board of directors who were in unanimous agreement that we should move forward slowly, one step at a time. One board member brought up some objections, but in the end, all ten board members voted to proceed.

As I look back, I had the sin of presumption. I *reasoned* that after twelve years of looking for the right property, this had to be from the Lord because we had never progressed so far in the permitting process or the approval by the county. I reasoned that the "Don't do the deal" voice must have been from the enemy—an attempt to thwart our progress through discouragement or distraction.

As human beings, we have brains in our heads to think and reason through every issue that we face. This ability to reason is truly a gift from God. However, our human logic can work against us when we don't take time to inquire of the Lord. We run off in a direction that He has not ordained. We oftentimes fail to realize that we have a loving God who does not operate in our time dimension and therefore sees what we cannot.

We started looking at the property in 2006 and finally closed the purchase in June of 2007, six months before the Great Recession was to set in. Although the recession had already started, most Americans didn't take notice until September of 2008 when Lehman Brothers failed. Like many other Americans, we bought the property at the top of the market when prices were still at the peak in 2007. We could not have chosen a worse time both to start a new ministry and buy a piece of property.

The primary reason we bought the property was because it had two houses located on it, which we could renovate and use for housing. In addition, the property had a forty-acre, income-producing orchard made up of apple, cherry, pear, and peach trees.

Needless to say, life does take its unique twists and turns. Never in my wildest dreams did I envision myself being an orchardist overseeing ten thousand fruit trees! Throughout my life, I have never had a green thumb; I only had a black thumb. Our home was considered by some to be a plant hospice—a place where plants would go to die. That should have been one of my first clues that maybe something wasn't quite right.

Life was extremely hectic. It was a season in my life that did not have much in the way of margin. In July of that year, I felt an urgency in my spirit. It was not a gentle nudge but a spiritual shove from the Holy Spirit. I felt Him saying to me, "You *must* fast this year!" Again, the still, small voice!

Every day brought another, even stronger nudge that said, "You *must* fast this year!" This word from the Lord was new for me. In the case of each of my previous extended fasts, there had never been a "must" associated with a fast. Not a week went by that the nudge did not grow stronger. I am normally not prone to procrastination; however, I was dragging my feet about the directive to complete a fast. I had many excuses: the short-term mission trips were occurring like clockwork, there were endless details to attend to in setting up the new aftercare facility, the day-to-day ministry operations of PFC had to be overseen, and support-raising had to occur for both ministries. My life was jam-packed.

At that time, Rhonda and I lived in our primary home on the west side of the mountains one week, and then we would pack up to go live in the small bungalow on the orchard the following week. It made for a lot of busyness, but we also had the best of both worlds—city life and country life.

As the summer of '07 wore on, I kept one eye on the calendar. I received a very ominous message in my spirit that once again said, "You *must* fast this year!" The heaviness that enveloped my spirit was enough to stop me in my tracks one afternoon. I immediately sat down in front of my computer to try to piece things together. I did not know what the purpose of the fast was to be, but I knew I needed to be "prayed up." I had two more short-term mission trips to complete that year. Fitting a forty-day fast into the remainder of the year was going to be like putting the pieces of a 3-D puzzle together—it was going to require a lot of precision.

I had three options. First, I could fast over one of my scheduled mission trips, which was not really an option at all. We were already battering our bodies under extreme conditions on these trips. Second, I could fast over the Thanksgiving or Christmas holidays. I'd been there and done that. It was not a fun situation, so in my mind, that was not even remotely possible! At that point I began asking myself, "How did I let myself become so boxed in like this?" The third option seemed to be the only viable one, to start the forty-day fast in between the Uganda and India trips scheduled for September and November. In order to have enough days before the India trip to reacclimate my stomach to food—no less the hot Indian food—I knew I would have to start the fast the day that I returned from Uganda.

I returned from Uganda on a Sunday in September. It was my third mission trip that year. On my way home, I drove to my favorite restaurant, Mickey D's! I ordered a Big Mac combo with an oversized Diet Coke and vowed that this meal would be my last one for the next forty days. Rhonda was not on the Uganda trip with me, but I had told her before leaving that an extended, long-term fast was in the making, and that I would most likely start it the day I got back from the trip.

In the first forty-day fast, all I had known was that I was to *stand in the gap* for the election. The second forty-day fast, I was instructed to partner with my wife. I also learned the lifelong principle of journaling and to be specific in my prayers for a fast. I had six specific prayer requests for the second fast. During the third forty-day fast, I excelled in my journaling and added eight specific, defined prayer requests—one of which was for the salvation of my dad.

Before the fourth fast, at the insistence of my wife, I went into the doctor's office to inform my doctor of over twenty years of my plans for an extended fast. My doctor knew about my first, second, and third fasts only after the fact. Each time his eyes got as big as saucers. He would then put his hand on my shoulder and remind me to check in with him before I started another extended fast. This would allow him to draw blood and establish a benchmark as to how well my body was doing.

The one thing different as I headed into my fourth extended fast (besides actually seeing the doctor first) was the why. All I remembered was the word from the Holy Spirit in the months prior: "You *must* fast this year!" This urgency, but with no clear reason, was very disconcerting to me.

Still, with three extended fasts under my belt, I knew what to expect… or so I thought.

The Message Revealed

I was prepared, I was prayed up, and I knew I was going to fast. It was the Sunday morning after I had crawled off a ten-hour flight from Amsterdam to Seattle. Because of jet lag, I was up and out of bed by four that morning. I knew this was the first of forty mornings that I would go without breakfast. I made my way downstairs to my favorite quiet-time chair and rested in the Lord, reflecting on the mountaintop experience of having been on the other side of the world less than twenty-four hours earlier. My quiet time soon turned into seeking God's face and direction for this fast.

In the previous three fasts, I had known on the first morning the purpose for each of them. For this fast, all I knew was that the still, small voice had been relentless in telling me, "You *must* fast this year." I cried out to the Lord to reveal Himself to me regarding the purposes for this fast. Soon the Lord spoke to me these words, "You are to fast to *stave off disaster.*" I was terrified by this directive. "I am to do what? To *stave off disaster?* What does that mean, Lord?"

I will let my journal entries tell the rest of the story. These are short excerpts from my journal notes.

Day One—Sunday, September 16, 2007

Oh Lord, I come to you this day beseeching you to give me strength. Send the ravens to spiritually feed and sustain me, my

146

Lord. Your spirit has prompted me to fast. I look forward to this but with fear and trembling. You have stirred in my heart to fast. You have given me four words by your spirit—to stave off disaster. I have no idea what that means, Lord. Does that mean personal disaster, family disaster, ministry disaster, church disaster, state disaster, or government disaster? What does that mean, Lord? You have given me this message. I stand firm and resolved to pray against this disaster. Bless you, Lord.

Day Two—Monday, September 17, 2007

Lord, this is so hard! Fasting is never easy, but so much harder when you are sick. (I am sick from the flu from the long airplane ride.) Lord, send your ministering angels to strengthen me. I *stand in the gap* for whatever is at stake. I pray up a hedge of protection around me, Rhonda, Ashley, Jaret, Dad, extended family, PFC, and the state and federal governments. Find me faithful, Lord, in this direction. Amen and amen!

Day Four—Wednesday, September 19, 2007

To stave off disaster! Those four words your Spirit has given me. I do not know what that means. I MUST stay the course. Please Lord, do not let me swerve to the right or to the left. Let me keep my eyes focused on you. Teach me Lord, how to *stand in the gap* for the message to stave off disaster. I count it an honor and a blessing to *stand in the gap* to stave off disaster. Find me faithful, oh Lord. When I am weak, you are strong.

Day Five—Thursday, September 20, 2007

To stave off disaster. Lord, what does that mean? This is a serious message you have given me. These four words are causing me great angst more than any of the surrounding life circumstances. You have chosen not to reveal this to me. Strengthen me to stay the course. With this day being day five of forty days, it seems all but impossible to stay the course. Be with me, Lord.

Day Twenty—Saturday, October 6, 2007

Oh, my Lord, I can't believe it is already day twenty. Sustain me, Lord. I do this fast to *stand in the gap* for something or somebody, in order to stave off disaster. I do not know what this message means. I may never know. What I do know is that this fast is from You for this time in my life. So I *stand in the gap* for someone or for others to stave off disaster.

Day Thirty-Nine—Wednesday, October 24, 2007

Two more days and five meals left, Lord. I praise you for sustaining me. This was the toughest fast yet, Lord. It must have been toughest because the message to pray and *stand in the gap* to stave off disaster must be imminent. Whatever that means, Your will be done. Praise be to the Lord, amen and amen, to God be the glory. Father, I have run the race, I have stayed the course, truly out of obedience for your direction to *stand in the gap* to stave off disaster. I still do not know what that means. If you chose to reveal the magnitude of that message, so be it, to your Glory.

I ended the fast the same way I had started it—not knowing the meaning of the message, *to stave off disaster.*

Bear up the hands that hang down, by faith and prayer; support the tottering knees. Have you any days of fasting and prayer? Storm the throne of grace and persevere therein, and mercy will come down.[43]

John Wesley

CHAPTER 15

Storm Clouds Ahead

THE FAST ENDED with my traditional meal of a couple of bites of meatloaf and a couple of bites of mashed potatoes. After each fast, there were mixed emotions. I never wanted to go back to the way things were in the physical realm, but I also knew that my body needed nourishment to continue to function. This particular fast was quite troubling in the beginning of the fast, during the fast, and as the fast ended. The message *to stave off disaster* was overwhelming. What that meant was never revealed to me during the fast. I was perplexed, a little anxious, and in a mental quandary. The message stuck to me as peanut butter sticks to a dog's tongue. It wouldn't go away. However, as normal life took over, the memories of the fast drifted further and further behind me.

The ministries of Prisoners For Christ were bursting at the seams in a good way. We had a staff of eight, and everyone was operating on all eight cylinders. Staff members knew their job assignments and were executing them well. Our outreach around the world was expanding in spite of the recession. However, the ministries of Standing Stones (the name we had given to our aftercare ministry) were not going nearly as well as those at PFC.

By Seattle's standards, 2008 was a difficult winter. This made for difficult weekly navigation of the mountain pass that divides Washington State into the eastern and western halves. It was physically and emotionally draining to traverse the mountain pass with so much ice and snow as we crossed the state from west to east and back again each week. Although the staff stability at PFC was great, staff stability at Standing Stones was not. It seemed as if we could not hold on to staff for very long. When an employee left, the absence caused the Von Tobels great stress as it meant we had to spend more than just every other week on the other side of the state. It added responsibilities to our already-full plates.

In the summer of 2008, I was starting to have some great concerns over the economy. At that time, no one even contemplated the severity of the recession. Having to raise support for two ministries in a good economy was a stretch, but having to raise monies for two ministries in a bad economy was quite the battle. In addition, I never thought that at the age of fifty-three I would be in a position where I had to learn so much about pruning, thinning, pesticides, and varmints. It seemed as if every day brought a new challenge and new learning experiences.

§

I was sitting in the airport in Amsterdam, waiting to board my Delta flight with my American team after coming back from a very successful trip to Nigeria in 2008, when my cell phone rang. It was Rhonda. "This can't be good," I thought to myself. She always knew exactly when my layovers were to occur, but she made a point to never call me during one. Her call at that time meant only one thing: a crisis unfolding. My heart was pounding out of my chest as I prayed no one had died or was in the hospital.

"Hello?"

"Hi, honey." It was always so good to hear her voice after being apart for so long.

"Hey there. How is everybody back home?"

"Everybody is fine, but I have some bad news I need to share with you. Are you sitting down?"

Oh my. She had never said that to me before: "Am I sitting down?" I said, "What's wrong?"

"Jill and I have talked. We thought we should tell you this before you hit the ground in Seattle."

"What now?"

"George and Mark are gone."

"What do you mean, they're gone? Gone where?"

George and Mark were my program directors at Standing Stones. George was in charge, and Mark was second in command. It turned out that George had left first, and then Mark left a day later. They packed their bags and just left with no notice or warning. They left with no one to oversee the men (all struggling with addictions), who were living in the house and going through the program.

Both George and Mark had been in varying stages of sobriety for several years before coming to Standing Stones. They had proven themselves capable at another program down south; therefore, I had reasoned that they would be good candidates for leadership in our fledgling ministry. Again, I had run ahead of the Lord when I had hired them. I had committed the sin of presumption and had not inquired of the Lord as to whether these were the right men for the job. I had reasoned within myself—but I had not asked the Lord for clear direction.

Both George and Mark had come through life with father-figure issues. When recovering addicts see life as too difficult, they run—and run they did, nowhere to be found. It came out later that George had met a woman on the Internet and decided to go live with her, giving up his God-ordained calling to minister to addicts. Mark had been overwhelmed by the news and left on a bus back to Florida the following day. Their departure once again left me with no margin, as I had to be on-site twenty-four hours a day until I found another program director. This was not a good way to end a mountaintop-mission-trip experience and certainly not a good way to start a new year.

By God's grace, through the financial reserves He had allowed us to have, we actually made it through the year for both ministries. On December 31, 2008, I went outside by myself and cried like a baby, thanking the Lord for sustaining us through that most difficult year.

At the start of 2009, I was quite certain it was going to be an even more difficult year for both of the ministries. The Great Recession showed no signs of letting up. I noticed that donations were beginning to slow at PFC, which is never a good thing for any ministry. I didn't know how

I could maintain cash flow for both ministries. The Lord kept bringing men to the program at Standing Stones. Some men stayed, and others left before their times were up. Regardless, ministry was happening, and men's lives were being touched by the Spirit of God.

Although it was one of the most physically and emotionally exhausting periods of my life, men's lives were being restored: husbands were being reconciled back to their wives and fathers back to their children. It was an all-time high as far as a personally rewarding time in my life. I was in the midst of helping men through some of the worst times of their lives. We would spend four hours in the morning seeking the Lord and working through the self-destructive cycles of drug and alcohol addictions. Each day men would openly weep in class as they were being touched by the hands and grace of our Father.

For ministry people, it is times like this that propel us forward to stay the course. However, on the flip side—the business side—there are the practical details of running a ministry, which cannot be ignored. The recession was deep, and it was painful. It seemed as if every day there was news of another ministry or nonprofit shutting the doors. I pondered how soon that would be us. Then it happened.

Tornado Hits—Four Dollars a Bin

The orchard business is a peculiar undertaking. Orchardists expend a lot of resources in time, energy, and money to raise a year's crop. However, they have to wait another year before being paid for their produce. I was told this; I was taught this. The concept was reiterated to me more than once. I understood it and thought I was prepared for it. In late summer of 2009, I was waiting for a check, which was payment for the apples we had produced in 2008. This was an all-important check, as I planned on using it to carry us through the rest of the year.

I sent one of the men in the program out to gather the mail at the end of our long driveway. There it was in the mailbox—our grower's statement with our check—the check that was to cover our needs for the remainder of 2009. My orchard foreman, Jose, taught me to go to the bottom of the statement to find how much we were to receive per bin. Jose told me that we needed to make at least one hundred dollars per bin just to break even. In 2008 we did just that. We more than broke even; we made a profit. That made me feel incredible!

However, my emotions had been set up for a crash. I was looking forward to some breathing room with a huge check this year too. I was expecting to make at least what we had made the prior year. My eyes went to the bottom of the page, and much to my horror, I saw four dollars per bin. My heart skipped a beat, and I quickly rationalized that there was a mistake. There was no way possible that we could have received a check for four dollars a bin. Somebody entered the wrong number and left off some digits.

I quickly filed it away, resolving not to become too stressed over something that was just a horrible mistake. I decided to wait until the next week, rationalizing that Mike, my fieldman from the fruit packer, would be able to explain and put my mind at ease.

Mike finally came by to check in on the 2009 production of our fruit trees. As we sat down, I slid the grower's statement over to his side of the table. I told him I didn't understand the four-dollars-per-bin number and asked him to please explain. There was silence—deafening silence. I felt the room start to spin. For the next hour I heard about the ins and outs of the orchard business and how the Great Recession was taking its toll. I was told that the bottom had fallen out of the orchard business. I listened to story after story of farmers throwing in the towel, some of whom had been in the orchard business for a lifetime. Some were voluntarily closing down, while others were being forced to close through bankruptcy.

Much of it made sense, but there was a whole lot that didn't. I was actually sick to my stomach once the meeting had ended. My mind was reeling. It was the first of many thoughts I would have of wanting to just get out. What had I done? Once again, I wanted a reboot, a do-over. I had no idea how we would survive the next month, let alone the remainder of the year.

As the days and weeks progressed, I started to see subtle changes occurring in the Lower Yakima Valley. Orchards that were once pristine and well-manicured were left unattended with the fruit still on the trees. It turned out that it was more expensive to pick the fruit than to just let it go and allow it to eventually rot off the trees. Apple trees were growing unkempt for lack of pruning. Once-productive orchards were not even being watered. I was shocked to see fruit hanging on the trees, waiting to drop to the ground and spoil.

I thought to myself, "Only in America would we let perfectly good fruit, food for someone, spoil on the tree." I reflected on all the trips I had made to foreign countries; scenes of malnourished children would flashback as in a horror film. I was repulsed that I was now ensnared in the system. I wanted out. I wanted to use my mulligan. To add to my disgust, I started seeing once-productive orchards being bulldozed and burned up, one after another. I thought to myself once again, "Only in America!"

Halfway through 2009, I got the only piece of good news for that entire year. My good friends, Dave and Gail Garton from Dunklin Memorial Camp, had decided to come to the Pacific Northwest and be the program directors for Standing Stones. Dunklin Memorial Camp, located in Okeechobee, Florida, is world-renowned for its work with addicts. It was founded by the late brother Mickey Evans and is run by another good friend, Hugh Murrow. For the previous ten years, Rhonda and I had been traveling down to Dunklin to see how they ran their successful recovery program.

Dunklin had set the bar high. They were the benchmark that we endeavored to replicate in the Pacific Northwest. At any one time, Dunklin would have between sixty-five and seventy men on-site in their recovery program. There were over thirty staff members assisting them in working out their addictive issues, which had caused so much pain in their lives. One of Dunklin's strong suits is that they are very family-friendly. They believe that a man in recovery needs to make amends for the past hurts that he has inflicted on his family. In their fifty-year history, hundreds of marriages have been—and continue to be—restored.

Rhonda and I were beyond elated about the prospects of Dave and Gail coming onboard. They were sound, they were stable, and they knew addiction-recovery programs. Dave Garton had a well-known and excellent reputation for the work he had done with addicts in the inner-healing process, both at Dunklin and around the world. On one of our trips down to Dunklin many years before, Rhonda and I had become instant friends with Hugh Murrow and his wife, Christy, along with Dave and Gail. I often thought we were kindred spirits. Having Dave and Gail come to Standing Stones would give Rhonda and me a much-needed break.

The Great Recession continued to wreak its havoc. I had no idea how I was going to pay this couple for the work they would be doing. We were out of money at the orchard, but in faith, we gave them the thumbs-up for coming to the Northwest. I told the board of directors that Dave and Gail were the canaries in the mine—that if they were to ever leave, it would mean closing down the program. This was not something any of us wanted to even consider. Rhonda and I were running out of steam. We had little emotional strength to step in to fill the holes that another departure of leadership staff would require. Dave and Gail's arrival came at God's perfect timing for the Von Tobels.

§

On December 31, 2009, Rhonda and I were at our daughter Ashley's in-laws' home. The year had gone by in a flash. Once again I made my secret pilgrimage outside, under the guise of needing some fresh winter air, to cry like a baby. I praised the Lord for allowing us to survive another year. It was truly a miracle that both ministries had survived the year without any major staffing cuts. I praised the Lord as tears streamed down my face.

Each year seemed to become progressively worse. I journaled about how I was amazed that we even survived 2008 and 2009. In my wildest imagination, I could not have conceived how either ministry would survive 2010. That year turned out to be an extremely painful year, more painful than the previous two years combined. It seemed as if every phone call was to inform me of another piece of farm equipment breaking down. On top of that, donations at Prisoners For Christ were crashing even more.

The Lord had taught me about fasting. Instead of doing another extended fast, I was prompted to fast two days a week for God's provision for both ministries. These two-day fasts were what really pushed me through those dark days. Depending on my schedule, some weeks I would fast on Monday and Thursday, other weeks it would Monday and Wednesday, and some weeks it would be two back-to-back days. I was fasting for survival. I was faithful throughout this time to carve out two days each week to fast.

As I shared earlier in the book, I have only broken a fast one time. That time occurred during this period in my life. I had a very busy week before me. I was having trouble figuring out how I would even insert two days of fasting in that week. I had already scheduled a lunch meeting with a new Christian farmer friend for Thursday of that week. I had determined that I would take him to lunch in town and have him order food for himself, but I would abstain. That was the plan. It was not necessarily an optimal plan, but it was one I had used many times when I was on an extended fast.

I pulled up to his farmhouse to pick him up. My friend came bounding out of the house with a great big grin on his face. He told me that he had talked his eighty-year-old mother into making a huge farm lunch for his family and me. Inside, I panicked. I had never broken a fast that I had committed to complete. But to fast in this situation would be extremely awkward and uncomfortable. However, having fasted through the Thanksgiving meal one year and multiple other important family functions, I was prepared to fast through this farmhouse lunch. I shot up a prayer for counsel from the Lord and asked Him what I was to do. In that still, small voice, the Lord said, "Eat what is placed before you." I was so grateful to the Lord.

For over a year, my foreman, Jose, had told me that if the orchard was to survive, I would need to take the fruit to the other side of the mountains to sell. I had no idea exactly what that would entail, but I was seriously considering doing it. I informed my fieldman in the fruit-packing house that they were not going to obtain all of our fruit that year. I let him know that I was going to take a third of the yield to sell on the other side of the state. He asked me, in a chiding and belittlingly way, "And how do you think you are going to do that?" My only response was, "I don't know, but when the time comes, the Lord will figure it out for me."

The time came. It was the middle of June, and the cherries were ready to be picked. I rented an air-conditioned Penske truck and started hauling cherries to the west side of the mountains. Six days straight, we operated almost seventeen hours a day driving the truck back and forth from one side of the state to the other. Much to my pleasant surprise, I couldn't keep the cherries stocked on my truck. One of the great incentives about this business model was that I didn't have to wait for the middleman to pay me. This was a "cash now" business. This extra revenue stream helped cover the expenses at Standing Stones over the next three months.

Next came the pear crop, the peach crop, and then the apple crop. I was shocked at how our fruit was selling through direct means. Yes, it was hard work. Yes, fruit does spoil, and yes, you need to harvest and sell it when it's ripe. In the same way a baby doesn't wait when he's ready to be born, fruit doesn't wait either. When it's ripe, it's ripe and needs to be sold. Selling the fruit directly bought us much-needed time to keep the doors open. It was all about serving the men in the program.

New men had come to Standing Stones in hopes of getting right with the Lord and overcoming their addictions. It was the day-to-day growth that I saw in these men that was the motivation I needed to push forward through this most painful financial recession. I kept telling myself that it was all about the men. I thought I was pouring into their lives, but they ultimately started pouring back into my life, unbeknownst to them.

"All In!"

In poker terminology, I was "all in." It was about survival, and I understood it. There was no plan B. However, I had made a monumental business miscalculation.

The Bible is clear: "No one can serve two masters" (Matthew 6:24). I had been spending almost 95 percent of my time working to keep Standing Stones alive. By this time, the "patient" was already intubated and on life support, but I didn't see it until it was too late. I had kept reminding myself that it was all about the men. Unfortunately, I had failed to give Prisoners For Christ, the mother ship, equal time. The recession was not subsiding; donations were falling through the floor. Then, it happened.

In August, my vice president of finance for PFC, Jill Payne-Holman, called me into her office and said, "I know you don't want to hear this, but I think we need to put the staff of PFC on part-time, or we are not going to make it through the end of the year."

The enormity of the situation finally crashed down around me. PFC, because of my lack of attention, was now suffering the consequences of that inattention. I knew Jill was right. I pay her to give me the cold, hard facts. She received no pushback from me. I hung my head. Silence—deafening silence—fell in the room…the silence that causes you to hear your own heart beating in your chest. Once again, I wanted out; I longed for a do-over. The ship was sinking right before my very eyes. How could I have let this happen? I informed the board through email that in order to survive for the rest of the year, we would need to put staff on part-time.

The following week, I made appointments with each staff member to tell them personally that we would have to cut their hours to part-time until the end of the year. I told them we would reassess the situation after the Christmas offering monies arrived at the end of December. If things didn't significantly turn around, then we would have to make deep and painful cuts after the first of the year. It was not a pleasant conversation, but everyone understood.

Throughout this time, I continued on with my fasting regimen, two days a week. As the weeks marched on, so did my resolve to be faithful in this spiritual discipline. I did not view fasting as a "genie in the bottle" nor think that I could move the hand of God because of something that I did. Fasting is not to be perceived as some magic formula. My prayers were for the Lord to carry me through this struggle according to His will. He did. He gave me strength, perseverance, resolve, and incredible peace—a peace that transcended all human experience. I knew I was in His hand. I felt Him every day. And I looked to please Him through this trial. Fasting opens the gates of heaven. I can't explain it, but something happens when you are fasting in the earthly that allows the heavenly to flow to the things of this life. This is why I have coined the term "heaven falls"!

The weeks and months trudged on with the recession still in full bloom. History tells us the Great Recession was over sometime in 2009. However, for nonprofits, the lingering effects continued on for another twelve to eighteen months. We had two more board meetings slated for September and November of 2010. Both meetings were consumed with the tyranny of the moment and how deep the cuts would have to be in order to survive. The board had instructed me to come up with a plan of action. I had never before done that. Since the ministry's inception, we had never seen a trial such as this one.

These were not pleasant board meetings. They were gut-wrenching meetings. We had sold enough fruit to sustain Standing Stones through the end of the year, but it was Prisoners For Christ that took the full brunt of the financial crisis. I reiterated to the board my thoughts on two subjects. First, if the Christmas offering didn't bring a significant increase, we would most definitely need to make cuts to the PFC staff. Second, if Dave and Gail Garton ever left the ministry, then we would need to shut down Standing Stones. Both points made for very sobering discussions.

The month of December is always a significant month for any nonprofit, as this is when extra donations come in that sustain the organization for the lean months that usually follow. The 2010 Christmas offering needed to be even larger than usual to avoid drastic staff cuts in January.

Things did not look good. So far, no increase in the usual end-of-the-year donations had been seen. It was hard to maintain a Christmas spirit. Three days before Christmas, our receptionist, Margaret, buzzed me to say that there was someone on the line who wanted to make a contribution to the ministry before the end of the year. I picked up the phone and exchanged pleasantries with a man whom I had never heard of nor met. He explained to me that he and his wife wanted to come in and meet with me between the holidays to discuss their potential donation.

The following week, I met with both of them at the PFC office. I learned that they had a trust fund that required them to make a disbursement before the end of the year, which was just a few days away. They were looking at several ministries as possible recipients. He had heard about PFC through a friend and wanted to meet me in order to consider the ministry. He was a businessman who was used to dealing with bottom lines. I shared my heart about Prisoners For Christ as well as Standing Stones, and that was it. As quickly as the meeting started, it ended. He informed me that he and his wife would discuss things and reconnect with me in the next day or two.

The next day brought no phone calls. I waited and prayed. I was anxious and wanted to call, but the Lord said no. Then on Wednesday, December 29, I received a call. The man told me that he had just put a check in the mail for $100,000, our second largest, single, one-time check to the ministry, to be used however needed. Two days before the end of the year, two days before major cuts to the ministry were to occur, the Lord Jesus Christ extended His hand of mercy to both ministries. We were able to put the staff at PFC back to full time the first week of January 2011.

I never saw that businessman again.

Woe to the fasting that leaves sin in our lives untouched...The hunger of fasting is a hunger for God, and the test of that hunger is whether it includes a hunger for holiness.[44]

John Piper

CHAPTER 16

The Orchard—My Friend, My Enemy

WE KNEW THAT $100,000 was truly a godsend. We were as frugal as we could be and made those funds last as long as possible. Although the government was claiming that the recession had ended, I was scratching my head. Had the recession really ended? The unemployment rate was still very high. Donations were inching up, but ever-so-slowly. I asked my peers if they felt that the recession had really ended. They all felt the same way that I did; we weren't quite out of the woods just yet.

One day I received a phone call from my dear friend Dave Garton, who was doing an exemplary job of holding things together on the program side at Standing Stones. He asked me when I was next coming to visit because he wanted to meet. I remember hearing a sense of urgency in his voice. I knew before he even told me; Dave was going to tell me that he and Gail were leaving the ministry. He hadn't yet said it, but I sensed in my spirit that was what he needed to tell me. The following week I met with him at one of our favorite business-meeting spots, the local Dairy Queen in Wapato. He stuttered and stammered for a few seconds until I said, "Dave, just go ahead and say it."

For the next few hours, two friends shared their hearts. He had agonized over the decision. He knew what it meant for the program if he and Gail left. I didn't blame Dave at all. Dave and Gail were my heroes. They were grossly underpaid. Combine that with the cold winters in Eastern Washington and being so far away from any family and friends—it's admirable they stayed as long as they did. They were ready to take off for their next God-ordained assignment. I was actually quite happy for them. However, for Standing Stones, it was checkmate, game over. The decision to close was final and firm. Because of my fasting, I was at peace…a surreal peace.

The last graduation of men from the program was in June of 2011. We found homes for the remaining men who had not yet graduated, bid our farewells to our good friends, and buttoned up Standing Stones for its first long winter with no one on-site. Before leaving one afternoon, I decided to take a walk out in the orchards. Throughout the few years that we had owned the property, I had oftentimes found great peace and solitude by going as deep as I could into the orchard and resting in the Lord.

The orchard was my "frenemy." I had a love-hate relationship with it. It brought me such pain just to keep it maintained, but then it brought me such incredible peace in the depths of despair. Peace with the Lord could be found during long walks among the endless rows of trees. Many a man had found his way back to the Lord on those solitary walks, walks that would change the course of a man's life.

The end was near. I knew the grieving process had already begun for what some call the "death of a vision." I had observed it in others who had trod this path, but had never experienced it firsthand. It was very painful, but at the same time, it was also very peaceful. Those two words seem to be such polar opposites—pain and peace. How could they coexist? They did. That is how I picture death—painful in the temporal but peaceful in the eternal.

While in the orchard, I contemplated the sale of the property. The land had been acquired at the peak of the market. Real-estate prices had fallen much lower, and I wondered how I could even sell it for enough to pay off the existing mortgage, much less the other outstanding expenses. I said to myself, "If I am not careful, this could turn out to be an utter disaster." As soon as the word *disaster* fell out of my mouth, I heard that still, small voice, that voice I hadn't heard in a long time, whisper in my spirit… *to stave off disaster.*

What? Oh no! It's happening again. I hadn't thought of those ominous-sounding words in almost four years. I had become too busy and distracted over the last several years to be concerned about those four words. Why was this happening again at this point in my life? I felt I had endured enough. At the beginning of the fourth fast, I hadn't known what those four words meant and still did not know their meaning once the fast ended. Now they came crashing down on my head. I dropped to my knees and cried out to the Lord for help.

Things were silent out in the far reaches of the orchard. The only noise I heard was from the occasional fly that would buzz close to my face. I finally had the answer to what I had questioned for so long: the purpose of the fourth fast was not for others—it was for me. What I *didn't* know was even more troubling. Had I just completed the trial, or was I moving into it with the force of a freight train? Almost as soon as the question formed in my mind, I was given the answer. As I walked out of the orchard, I felt at peace that *to stave off disaster* was not for what I had just endured, but for what was forthcoming!

I was now forced with a very difficult set of decisions. There were no men in the program, therefore we had no program fees as revenue. To stop the bleeding in 2010, we decided to lease the orchard land to a local farmer. The arrangement was that he paid for all of the expenses of running the orchard, and in lieu of rent, he would pay us a small percentage of the revenue stream from the sale of the fruit. Once again, the revenue stream that we needed *now* would come a year down the road, leaving us with no immediate income from the fruit.

On top of all that, I had no donations coming in. I could not ask donors to give money to a nonexistent program. I felt dead—dead in the water. I couldn't go forward and couldn't go backward. My back was up against the wall. Having absolutely no options to exercise was a new experience for me. In my life, there were always options…but not this time. The Lord had always gifted me with the ability to see multiple options for any decision path, but that was not the case this time. It was a true disaster in the making: nothing coming in and bills stacking up.

Rhonda and I did have some equity in our home. Would I sacrifice those funds? Could I even ask my wife to do such a thing? There was one other alternative: turn the property back to the bank and allow it to be foreclosed upon—just walk away. That thought crossed my mind many times. It was quite tempting. I could rationalize that everyone else in the country was doing it. That was the easy way out, but not paying my bills was not in my DNA. Filing for bankruptcy was not for me—idea squashed! Two words that I had never allowed to cross my mind as alternatives to hard situations were *divorce* and *bankruptcy*. They are not in my vocabulary. To entertain those thoughts would be the beginning of compromise.

Thoughts of compromise sneak up on you, but of course never when things are going well. No, they work their way in when things are going poorly. They start planting their destructive seeds when the costs are high. They are subtle. In order to be able to fight compromise, you must be ready to identify it and speak against it from its inception.

The darkest days of this ordeal came when I took Rhonda out for dinner to lay out my thoughts and feelings. I told her that if this got ugly, really ugly, and I couldn't sell the farm for more than enough to pay off the mortgage and the bills, and to make everyone whole, then we would need to sell our house and use the equity to meet those obligations. I told her if it came to that, I would buy her the best tent I could afford, a can of paint, and some materials for window coverings so she could make her new nest with the Rhonda flare. Rhonda then did what she does best. She threw me her signature smile and said, "The Lord knows; you and He will figure this out."

The next week, with a renewed sense of confidence, I pulled out the journal of my fourth fast in 2007 and reread it. While sipping a hot cup of coffee, I spent the next couple of hours reading and remembering the blessings of that fast. Once I finished reading the journal, a strange peace came over me. I had done what the Lord had instructed me to do. "You must fast this year" for the purpose *to stave off disaster.* If God had instructed me to fast four years before I was knee-deep in this trial, then I knew that I was in the palm of His hand. I knew what lay ahead was going to be most difficult and ugly. However, I was very much at peace.

Another challenge I had was to find a real-estate agent who would be willing to take on the daunting job of selling an orchard in a real-estate environment where other orchards were being auctioned off for pennies on the dollar. As I mentioned, we had bought this property at the peak of the real-estate market in 2007. We needed to recoup our money to pay off the remaining mortgage balance, as well as all the other outstanding expenses. Taking a loss was not an option. I finally found a broker who was willing to take on this unenviable task. He made no bones about the fact that he thought this was a select, but difficult, piece of property with some potential to sell. But he would not commit to how long he thought that sale might take.

I quickly asked Jill, my vice president of finance, to calculate what I needed to pay the current bills. It came to around $3,000 per month. How was I going to find $3,000 per month without any income sources? Rhonda and I had nothing in our savings account. I couldn't ask donors to throw good money after bad—a lesson learned from my previous stock-broker days. We listed the property going into the holiday season, definitely not the ideal time to sell an orchard. The winter was brutal that year, with very cold days and lots of what they call "freezing fog" in the Lower Yakima Valley. This made for horrible driving conditions.

No one was making the trek to visit an orchard fifteen miles out of town during that kind of weather. Three months went by with very little activity on the property. I decided to give the agent one last shot and renewed our contract for another three months. This extension moved us into the spring with the hopes of increased activity and interest in the property, but to no avail. The thought of having to find a new agent made my stomach churn. Another delay; another failure. However, I knew what I needed to do. I politely fired our current agent and went looking for "new blood." I selected my second choice of realtors from the original pool I had considered six months prior and signed on with her.

My New Best Friend—Craigslist

During those dark winter months, the Lord gave me a couple of ideas. We had lots of essential and nonessential equipment at the orchard. I decided that I would test the waters of Craigslist, something I had never before done. Sure enough, things started to sell, one by one. At one point, Jill said I was selling everything that wasn't nailed down. Additionally, while in the throes of cutting expenses at the orchard, we had previously decided to bulldoze down about ten acres of old-style apple trees, trees that produced the kinds of apples that no one was buying. Once this was done, we allowed some of those trees to just sit on the ground. Someone had the idea that we could market the applewood and sell applewood chips. Although this idea did not take off, we were able to sell cords of wood.

Much like I am so *not* an orchardist, I am so *NOT* a mechanic. I don't even remember how this began, but I was introduced to car auctions. I started going to these auctions and would buy one to two cars at each auction. I would then clean them up and flip them for a small profit. It was similar to the way one might buy and flip a house. It was in the heat of the recession. People were not buying new cars; they were buying used cars, and the used-car market was hot.

All these small little revenue sources equaled $3,000 each month. When we were light some months, God's ravens would feed us by dropping surprise checks in our laps. I am reminded of the time that we received a check for $800 for a Labor and Industries overpayment that we had made several years back. This was God's forced-saving plan, which we didn't know anything about. Other times, we received a trash bill refund, an unemployment overpayment refund, and once, even an unexpected check from previous fruit sales.

From the time we put the orchard up for sale to when we sold it was approximately sixteen months—sixteen months of no revenue stream, but sixteen months of paying the bills, $3,000 per month, or $48,000 total. No bill was late, and each month, the mortgage payment was made on time.

When talking about miracles, some people want empirical data. I just can't give it. God was incredibly faithful.

Once again I found myself waist-deep in miracle territory. Being in miracle territory wasn't new for me, but the length of time I was there was a very new experience. I remember miracle after miracle. There were many struggles in those sixteen months after the program shut down. Some relationships were strained with those who thought I should be doing things this way or that way. Friendships were sometimes tested. However, I stayed the course and stayed true to what I believed the Lord was leading me to do: to owe no man any debt.

In February of 2013, the property was finally sold, the papers were signed, and the orchard was no longer ours. The mortgages were paid in full. My God had been faithful in a very supernatural way. I had purposed in my heart that when all was said and done, no friend, no vendor, and no bank would lose money on this deal. I was committed to this principle even to the point of losing our home. That firm conviction, coupled with the fourth extended fast—God moved mightily on my behalf. He went before me and was my rear guard. Fasting gave me humbleness of heart. It gave me an incredible peace that I had never experienced before, and it gave me great confidence that the Lord was fighting my battles for me. Realizing that God had prepared the way for me four years prior by prompting me with the words "You must fast this year" humbles me to my core. The God that I love, loved me enough to prepare a way for me and prepare my heart for trials to come, even before I was in the thick of them.

The God that loves me, loves you. If God will do that for me, what will He do for you?

I have had inmates, as well as free men, come to me and say, "But preacher, you don't know what I have done. You don't know my thoughts. How can this God love me as He loves you?" Maybe you are even thinking the same thing. You know, you are right—in one aspect. I don't know what you have done or what you are thinking about doing, but this I know: I serve a loving God who cares for His children. He will meet you in your addiction. He will meet you at your weakest point. Trust in Him, in Him alone. His Word is full of promises. What are you going to do?

$\int$

There are three categories of people who are reading this book.

1. Those who have never placed their trust in Jesus.
2. Those who have backslidden from the faith.
3. Those who know the Lord intimately.

To those who have never placed their trust in Jesus, I say to you, time is short. No man knows the day or time that he will be called upon to give an accounting of his life before a holy and righteous God. I say to you, don't wait. Do it now! Ask for forgiveness of your sins, and ask Jesus into your life. If that is your heartfelt desire today, then please pray this prayer in the quietness of your heart:

Lord Jesus, please come into my life. I ask forgiveness of all my past sins, all my present sins, and all my future sins. I ask you Jesus to come into my life in a powerful way as my Lord and Savior of my soul. Be there with me as the trials of life come my way. Carry me over troubled waters, and teach me your ways. Oh God, have mercy on me today.

If you prayed to receive Jesus, you will now need to seek out a good Bible believing church in your local area where you might grow in understanding God's word and His purpose for your life.

If you fall into category two, if you are a backslidden Christian and someone has given you this book because of the trials and struggles they see in your life, I say to you as well, time is short. Fall on your face *now*, and ask Jesus to forgive you of your backslidden state. Ask Him to come into your life in a powerful way. Ask forgiveness for your sins and start afresh.

Use this book as a fresh beginning, as you learn firsthand the power of fasting. Determine to fast one day a week to seek His face and His will for your life. Take one day at a time. Look to Him to help you do the right things and stop doing the wrong things. Learn to make correct decisions. Put compromise out of your mind. Fight the good fight.

If you are an active Christian, living out your life in these turbulent times, to you, my brother or sister, I say, fall prostrate before God beseeching Him to teach you how to fast for any struggles or addictions you are battling. Press into the Lord during your quiet times, and bond tightly to Him. Nail pride to the cross. Humble yourself before a holy and awesome God.

True spiritual revival will transcend anything we have ever experienced. It will change the way we think about ourselves, our God, our present, and our future...True revival will be akin to spiritual seismic activity, shaking us to our core, allowing us to see the profound overtake the profane, with the promise that our lives will never be the same.[45]

Ronnie W. Floyd

CHAPTER 17

—— § ——

Got Problems?

YEARS AGO THERE was an ad campaign that started with "Got Milk?" It was quite humorous. The Got Milk? advertising campaign "was created by the advertising agency Goodby Silverstein & Partners for the California Milk Processor Board in 1993 and was later licensed for use by milk processors and dairy farmers."[46] The campaign began in 1993 and just recently was discontinued in January of 2014. Over the years, those two words have taken on many different meanings. I recently saw a truck that said "Got Junk?" Another said "Got Sand?"

How about this one: "Got Problems?" I know you do. It seems as if the majority of Christians have some type of crisis they are dealing with today. It seems as if the Great Restrainer, the Holy Spirit, is being withdrawn from this world, thus allowing sin to run unchecked. What are you struggling with? I look around, and in this world there is great fear. At the time of this writing, Ebola in America is front and center, the stock market is crashing, ISIS is gaining ground, and enterovirus is sickening our infants. On top of that, our families are fractured, marriages are being dissolved, family businesses are failing, cancer is running rampant, and AIDS and Alzheimer's are killing people around the world.

What about you? What are you struggling with? Is your marriage on the rocks? Do you have a child who has informed you that he or she is gay? Has your only daughter come home and told you she is two months pregnant? Is your business failing? Is the IRS garnishing your wages? Did the rent check bounce? I once had a pastor say, "You are either in a trial, coming out of a trial, or about to enter into one." How true that is! Jesus said, "In this world you will have trouble" (John 16:33). Also, in James 1:2, the Bible says,

Consider it pure joy, my brothers, whenever you face trials of many kinds, because you know that the testing of your faith develops perseverance. Perseverance must finish its work so that you may be mature and complete, not lacking anything.

Today, many in the church in America cannot embrace this scripture about facing trials with joy. It is in our human nature to avoid anything that might cause us great pain. I understand that. I get it. However, I know in my own life that trials of many kinds have matured me into the man that I am today. Let us not shy away from the difficulties that come our way. Instead, let us allow God to teach us and challenge us through these experiences. A consistent prayer life, coupled with the discipline of fasting, will help you through the trials that will inevitably come in life. How will you accept your next crisis?

Let me tell you the story of a man I met at the Correctional Ministries and Chaplains Association convention in the summer of 2013 at Wheaton College. His name is Christopher Yuan. Christopher, along with his mom, Angela, and his father, Leon, were some of the keynote speakers at this prison ministry conference. Christopher Yuan was born the son of Chinese immigrants. Growing up in his Chinese household was most difficult. There was an expectation for achievement in this family. Neither of Christopher's parents knew the Lord, so the home was not a Christ-centered home. Life in the house was bad at best.

I was captivated by their life story as they were speaking at the convention. I was on the edge of my seat as they, with brutal honesty and transparency, shared their family's history. Many times you could have heard a pin drop in the auditorium as they laid bare their hearts and souls to a room full of strangers. Then Christopher's mom said something that propelled me to the very edge of my seat. She told the audience that she had fasted for her son's salvation. Fasting! Connection!

Being one who understood the power of fasting and was already halfway through the completion of writing this book, I wanted to hear more. They continued to share from their hearts story after story. Angela described one of Christopher's trips home from college. His parents had a suspicion that something was not right with Christopher and had wondered if their son was gay. One evening at the dinner table, Christopher exploded into a frenzy of shouting. He finally confessed to his parents that he was gay. Afterward, he stomped out of the house and returned to college.

While attempting to make sense of her son's confession to being gay, Angela decided she was going to commit suicide. Before taking this terrible step, she wanted to see her son one last time, so she made a trip to his college for a visit. Before she started the trip, she sought counseling and was given a Christian tract where she read the promise "Nothing can separate us from the love of God that is in Christ Jesus."[47] Those words changed her life, and in the subsequent weeks, Angela came to know Jesus as her Lord and Savior.

As Christopher's mom was coming to grips with her newfound faith in Jesus Christ, his world was spinning out of control. He capsulizes his life of drug-dealing and the gay lifestyle in a few short sentences from their book *Out of a Far Country: A Gay Son's Journey to God. A Broken Mother's Search for Hope*:

> I was spiraling down into a place I had never experienced before. The dark haze of depression colored my days and nights, and I tried to shake it by smoking more ice. The drugs I bought to sell ended up in my pipe. I was starting to go without sleep for up to ten days, strung out on ice. Then my body would finally collapse, and I'd sleep for one or two days straight.[48]

> Smoking ice made me desire sex more than food, so I started frequenting bathhouses. A bathhouse exists for only one reason: anonymous sex between gay men. It's typically a back-alley, hole-in-the-wall kind of place. I'd always go alone—no one goes there to socialize. [49]

I'd often lie to myself, saying that I'd just stop in for a moment and leave after one encounter. But eight hours—and countless, nameless faces—later, I was at the desk paying thirty dollars for another eight hours.[50]

The concern for their son's well-being was all-consuming for Angela and Leon. From a mother's perspective, she often prayed, "Lord, do whatever it takes to bring this prodigal son out of that far country to you."[51] She began fasting every Monday for her son. Upon returning from one particular trip to see Christopher, she decided to do an extended juice fast, which lasted thirty-nine days. Angela was persistent with her prayers before the Almighty—much like the widow and the judge found in Luke 18.

In a previous chapter of this book, I referenced the four different styles of fasting, in which I describe the *standing in the gap* fasting style. This is a fast where one takes up the spiritual task of travailing in prayer and fasting for someone who cannot fast for themselves, whether it is a sick person, an addicted person, an unbelieving family member, or a God-hater. Earlier in this book, I spoke of *standing in the gap* for my father, who, at the age of ninety-one, came to know Jesus. In the next chapter you will hear the story of Joe, who had no one to *stand in the gap* for him—what a pity to have no one interceding on your behalf.

There are many prodigals in the world today who have no one to *stand in the gap* for them. Christopher had one person—his mother. Angela writes in their book:

I'll stand in the gap for Christopher. I'll stand until the victory is won, until Christopher's heart changes. I'll stand in the gap *every day, and there I will fervently pray. And, Lord, just one favor, don't let me waver. If things get quite rough, which they may, I'll never give up on that son, nor will you. Though the Enemy seeks to destroy, I'll not quit as I intercede, though it may take years. I give you my fears and tears as I trust every moment I plead.[52]*

God's hand of protection was all over Christopher. Christopher was ultimately busted by the DEA. During his trial, he was looking at a sentence of ten years to life. He was found guilty and sentenced to seventy-two months in the federal prison system for drug trafficking. Through normal blood testing in prison, he was informed that he had been diagnosed HIV-positive. As he was lying in his bunk one evening, he noticed that another convict had scratched on the upper bunk these words: "If you are bored, read Jeremiah 29:11."[53]

Christopher went on a frantic search to find a Bible. He miraculously happened to find a Gideon Bible in the very bottom of a locker in his cell. He started reading Jeremiah 29:11, and his eyes fell on the words "a hope and a future." You see, when people go to prison, they often experience the reality of having no hope left in this life. When inmates read the Bible, which says, "Plans to prosper you and not to harm you, plans to give you a hope and a future," those words jump off the page and are illuminated as if there is a heavenly spotlight shining down upon the letters.

Christopher adds, "The thought that God could restore me and bring me back from captivity resonated deeply within my spirit. At this point, the world would be happy for me to be locked away for good. And yet, God was saying something completely different."[54]

In his search of the Bible, he came to know Jesus as his personal Lord and Savior. He then went on a search of the Bible for scriptures that could justify following Jesus and leading a homosexual lifestyle. When all he found were scriptures that condemn this behavior, he sought out the chaplain for counsel. The chaplain actually gave him a book teaching that the Bible does *not* condemn homosexual behavior.

This was Christopher's reaction:

> But as I started reading the book and reading the Bible passages it referred to, God's Holy Spirit convicted me that the assertions from that book were a distortion of God's truth. Reading His Word, I couldn't deny His unmistakable condemnations of

homosexual sex. I wasn't even able to get through the first chapter of that book, and I gave it back to the chaplain.

After that I turned to the Bible alone and went through every verse, every chapter, every page of scripture looking for biblical justification for homosexuality. I couldn't find any. I was at a turning point, and a decision had to be made. Either abandon God to live as a homosexual—by allowing my feelings and sexual passion to dictate who I was. Or abandon homosexuality—by liberating myself from my feelings—and live as a follower of Jesus Christ.[55]

Christopher chose to stand on God's authoritative Word. He started attending Bible studies in prison. He began to grow in the knowledge of the Lord. Because his growth became evident to others, he was oftentimes asked to deliver a sermon to the prison church.

Through God's miraculous hand, Christopher went to a sentence-reduction hearing, and much to his surprise, the judge reduced his sentence from six years to three years or thirty-six months. With good time served, another five months was subtracted off his sentence for a total sentence of thirty-one months. Christopher was aware of God's hand of mercy intervening in his life as he reflected on the fact that thirty-one months is a huge difference from the seventy-two months he was given at sentencing. This was a "Red Sea miracle" of his original ten years to life.

One of the Christian inmates challenged Christopher with a question. "Have you ever thought about being a preacher or a minister?"[56] Through the subsequent soul-searching that occurred because of that question, Christopher decided to apply to Moody Bible College while he was still sitting in prison. On the application form for enrollment to Moody, the college asked for three references from people who had known him as a Christian for one year. His mother wrote, "Christopher didn't have many choices in the prison at Lexington. He was finally able to persuade a prison chaplain, a prison guard, and another inmate to write references for him."[57]

Really? A prison chaplain, a prison guard, and an inmate are the only three references he could muster. From the human standpoint, this might look pretty bleak. However, we should remember two things. First, man looks at the outward appearances, but God looks at the inside. Second, when you have found favor with the Almighty, nothing is impossible.

In March of 2001, Christopher turned in his application to Moody Bible College. In the spring of 2002, Christopher moved to the campus of Moody Bible College. Four years later, he graduated with a bachelor's degree in Bible with an emphasis in music and biblical language. He graduated from Wheaton College in 2007 with a master of arts. He later was asked by Moody Bible College to teach part-time as an adjunct instructor in the Bible department. He is now attending Bethel Seminary in St Paul, Minnesota, where he focuses his studies on sexuality and celibacy.

What an incredible story of a redeemed life. No fictional author could have ever scripted the outcome of this man's life: only the great Author and Perfecter of our faith, Jesus Christ. As I read the book *Out of a Far Country*, I was amazed by the depths of Christopher's depravity. There is neither enough time nor space in this book to explain further. As a man of God, I personally would have gone so far as to say that this man, based on all outward appearances, was beyond the reachable. I would have gone so far as to say this man had crossed the line—not able to reason right from wrong or the holy from the unholy according to God's Word.

However, the good news is that we serve a truly awesome God: "Man looks at the outward appearance, but the Lord looks at the heart" (1 Samuel 16:7). This testimony goes to show you that God's love can penetrate the darkest of hearts. God's light reached through to the thief on the cross—it has reached through the darkness to the Ted Bundys of the world, it has reached through to Mark David Chapman (John Lennon's killer), it has reached through to David Berkowitz (Son of Sam killer), it has reached through to Karla Faye Tucker—it even reached through to Jeffrey Dahmer, as well as to Christopher Yuan. It has reached through to me in my depravity as it has reached through to you. There is no one unreachable. However, there are many who cannot *stand in the gap* for themselves.

Christopher had two things going for him. He had a God who loved him unconditionally, and he had a mother who did not give up in travailing in prayer for her son.

Fasting is the way of denying self and experiencing greater measures of holiness. It causes you to be more real with God. Suddenly it becomes clear what is holy and what is unholy.[58]

Dave Williams

CHAPTER 18

The Rocket Launcher

Got problems? I know you do. Kids are going sideways. Accidents happen. Relationships are strained. Houses are being foreclosed upon. Jobs are being lost. Brain tumors are being discovered. Car engines are blowing up. Identities are being stolen. Pornography can be accessed on smart phones. Hackers are hacking. Husbands are having affairs. Wives are having affairs. Kids are overdosing. College women are being date-raped. Planes are going down. ISIS is on the move. New viruses are being discovered. Home invasions are happening. Children are bearing children. Fathers are leaving their posts. Kids are killing kids in schools. Christians are being martyred and imprisoned around the world for their faith. Sharia law is coming to the United States…on and on and on. It seems as if the wheels are coming off the world, and they are.

What are you going to do? How are you going to survive in this world? How are you going to protect your family in a world that is self-destructing before your very eyes?

Let's take a closer look at the Christopher Yuan story. There were four practical things that stood out to me that Angela did on behalf of her son.

1. Prayer

We are in a spiritual battle. We know that…or at least we *should* know it. Ephesians 6:12 tells us, "For our struggle is not against flesh and blood, but against the rulers, against the authorities, against the powers of this dark world and against the spiritual forces of evil in the heavenly realms." Saints, we are in a battle for our lives, for our families' lives, and for our spiritual well-being. God has not left us alone without any weaponry. He has outfitted us for battle. Therefore, we are to put on the full armor of God. Are you putting on the full armor of God every day? Ephesians 6:18 says, "And pray in the Spirit on all occasions with all kinds of prayers and requests. With this in mind, be alert and always keep on praying for all the saints."

Prayer is the number one weapon in our arsenal of spiritual weaponry. We must learn to use it effectively and efficiently; otherwise we will be adrift on the raging seas. Momma Angela excelled in this area of spiritual discipline. She prayed for her son. She had a shower in her home converted to her secret prayer closet. There, she would do business with God, travailing in prayer for her son and her family.

2. Standing in the Gap

Ezekiel 22:30 says, "I looked for a man among them who would build up the wall and stand before me in the gap on behalf of the land so I would not have to destroy it, but I found none." Let me share with you again the prayer from Angela on behalf of her son:

> *I'll stand in the gap for Christopher. I'll stand until the victory is won, until Christopher's heart changes. I'll stand in the gap every day, and there I will fervently pray. And, Lord, just one favor, don't let me waver. If things get quite rough, which they may, I'll never give up on that son, nor will you. Though the enemy seeks to destroy, I'll not quit as I intercede, though it may take years. I give you my fears and tears as I trust every moment I plead.*[59] (Emphasis added.)

Christopher had a mother who would not let go of the hope for her son's salvation. What does it mean to *stand in the gap* for someone? It means never letting go of hope. It means you will do spiritually whatever it takes at whatever the cost for that individual—and never give up! It means that you are the twenty-first-century version of the widow in the parable found in Luke 18:1–5. This is a powerful parable of a judge who did not fear God or man, but because the widow continued bothering him, he granted her request. Let us be found faithful in never giving up our intercession for a loved one.

Standing in the gap for others typically means that they are no longer able to *stand in the gap* for themselves. In Christopher's case, he was in full-blown rebellion. He was a God-hater. He wanted nothing to do with God or His holy Word. He was turning into a degenerate; his mind was being scorched. He hated his parents and everything for which they stood. He was being held tightly in Satan's grip, and there was no way out for this young man except through a mother's cry of compassion and for her son to turn to God.

Who do you know that is a God-hater? Is there someone in your family who is in full-blown rebellion? Will you *stand in the gap* for that person? As I pointed out previously, many who are so far from God cannot *stand in the gap* for themselves.

I am reminded that in my first fast, the Lord asked me a question in my spirit the morning after the election: "Will you *stand in the gap* for this country?" I said yes, never thinking that it would lead to a forty-day fast. The first fifteen days were a pity party, which I have since confessed. The latter half of the fast was when heaven fell. It was all about what I was called to do, to humble myself, before a holy and righteous God, to *stand in the gap* for that election and this country.

In the third fast, I was *standing in the gap* for my father's salvation. My father was a good man...a sweet man, and I am honored to be his son. However, he did not know Jesus and time was running out. He was in his late eighties, and he could have died instantly at any time. I *stood in the gap* for his eternal salvation. He couldn't do it himself. Dad wasn't like Christopher in one sense: he wasn't a God-hater. But he was risking his eternity by not putting his trust in Jesus.

Who do you know like my dad who needs to come to Jesus—someone in your family, someone at your office, maybe it is even your spouse? Then commit to fast for that person one day a week. Pity the man who has no one to *stand in the gap* for him!

Joe

Let me share a story with you of someone who had no one to *stand in the gap* for him. On my way into the office one day, I stopped by the local Safeway store in Duvall for my breakfast of champions—a large Diet Coke and two doughnuts. It was a typical Northwest fall day, maybe fifty degrees with the rain blowing sideways. I had my hoodie up as I approached the entrance. I noticed two lumps of clothes half-underneath the overhang, off to the side of the main entrance. I thought it was quite strange, as I had never seen anything like that in all the years I had been going to Safeway. I became horrified as I got closer and realized those two lumps of clothes were worn by an actual body.

As I approached, I reasoned it was an older Hispanic man lying face-down with foam coming out of his mouth. He had shallow breathing and was shivering in the driving rain. I called 911. As I waited for the paramedics to come, I observed that this man had on a dirty white, short-sleeve shirt on this wet and chilly day. I wondered who this man was and what his life story must have been. How could a man at this age end up like this? I gently talked to him about Jesus and prayed over him. His eyes were barely open, and he could not respond to any of my questions. I attempted to comfort him the best I could with the words the Lord gave me. I felt bad that I didn't have a blanket to cover him.

Minutes later the paramedics rolled up with lights flashing and sirens screaming. As they piled out of their bus, one paramedic looked at the other and exclaimed, "It's Joe!"

Excuse me? It's Joe? It was obvious that they had been called to service him more than once. This caused me to ponder even more as I wondered about his life. Pity the man who has no one to *stand in the gap* on his behalf.

Dave Williams, in his book *The Miracle Results of Fasting*, answers the question regarding fasting for others:

Can we fast for others? Yes! Fasting is one of the most powerful things we can do on someone's behalf. Most people have never heard of George McCluskey. He was a man of God who had two daughters and one son. One day he decided that he was going to skip his lunch daily and spend that time praying for his children. In the course of time, his two girls married ministers and his son went into the ministry. Pretty soon they started having children, and George decided to fast for his grandchildren and future great-grandchildren, too.

The grandchildren grew up and went to college. All of the girls married ministers and missionaries, and all of the boys went into the ministry or were preparing to go into the ministry except for one rebel who chose psychology, even though he felt guilty about it. He thought he was ruining a family tradition because everyone else had gone into the ministry, but his heart kept pulling him to psychology.

Today that "rebel" has several best-selling books that help parents raise their children in a Christian way. His name is Dr. James Dobson, and his career began with a fasting and praying grandfather![60]

3. QUIET TIMES

Quiet times are another weapon in the arsenal of believers. However, this weapon is becoming less and less used by Christians today. When I first became a Christian, all I heard about was quiet times and how important they were to our spiritual well-being. In the beginning of my walk with Christ, my quiet times were nonexistent. Eventually they became sporadic and then grew to the point of becoming a *must*. Just as exercise is a *must* for some people, so are my quiet times for me.

My quiet times are four to five times per week. I cannot survive without these times with the Lord in the morning. Given the state of the world, I honestly can't imagine how anyone survives without quiet times. They are where I obtain my strength. Like Samson received his strength from his hair, I receive my daily strength from my quiet times. They are precious to me. I seek the Lord, read His Word, send prayers up on behalf of the ministry and others, and find comfort in the Master's arms.

In my position as president of a ministry, I have a lot of lunch appointments with members of our constituency. The people I know particularly well, I often ask an accountability question. "How are your quiet times doing?" Many hang their head and mumble that they could be better, which means they are basically nonexistent. Rarely do I find those who say their quiet times are great. On the rare occasion that I do find someone who is having great quiet times, it feels as if two long-lost brothers have been reunited. Both of our faces light up as we share what a blessing it is to have intimate fellowship with the Lord.

When I was fasting, my quiet times hit new highs. Times of fasting propelled me to an even closer intimacy with the Lord. The longer I fasted, the greater the desire was for a deep, fervent, and protracted prayer time with the Lord.

In Christopher's case, he had a mother who understood the power of the quiet time. It was in these times that she had with the Lord, in her makeshift shower, that she labored in prayer for her son's salvation. Her quiet times became her strength. Do you desire that kind of spiritual strength? Dig deep inside of yourself and make a commitment to have a quality quiet time. There is no better time than now to start planning.

4. The Rocket Launcher

Modern-day soldiers have many weapons at their disposal. Their number one weapon while on patrol is their automatic rifle. They also have pistols, grenades, knives, and other assorted weapons. However, their weapon of choice is their rifles, because this is the weapon that kills their enemy. They are seen carrying them every day. They clean their rifles; they take care of their rifles. Some even sleep with their rifles. Their rifles must perform, or else they are dead. A soldier without a rifle is a dead soldier. That statement has been drilled into their heads since boot camp, where they are taught how to meticulously clean and care for their rifles.

Another tool of the professional soldier is the shoulder-fired rocket launcher. It is much different from the rifle. It has a different purpose. Where the rifle is used every day, the rocket launcher is not. Where the rifle is used to kill the enemy, the rocket launcher is used to blow up targets. It is used primarily to penetrate buildings, structures, and tanks, thus killing the enemy in hard-to-access spots. The rocket launcher is used for specific purposes. It is much heavier to carry, and the ammo is much more powerful. Much like the rifle, the rocket launcher also must be maintained and treated with care.

In the spiritual army, prayer is the rifle. We carry it around every day. We understand it, we take care of it, and we use it. This weapon is what kills the enemy and his schemes. Fasting, however, is the rocket launcher in the spiritual arsenal. The problem today with this spiritual rocket launcher is that very few Christians know how to use it. Many are never taught how to use it, and therefore, are afraid to use it. Few understand it, so they leave it in the bunker, only to collect dust and sit idle. Rocket launchers are meant to be used, not to sit around and collect dust. A weapon that sits around and collects dust is of no value to its soldier.

Some of us are not only ignorant, we are flat-out lazy. We don't want to know about our rocket launchers, nor do we want to engage them. We are fat babies sitting on the couch of life, crying over trivial matters that have no eternal consequences. We haven't looked into our weapons bunker in years. What's worse is that we have allowed our prosperity to become a sin. Our wealth has become idols in our lives.

Did you know Jesus had something to say about rocket launchers? Let's check out what Jesus said about these modern-day rocket launchers!

In chapter 9 of the book of Mark, the first few verses detail the story of the transfiguration. Jesus and His disciples Peter, James, and John are on a mountaintop where Jesus is transfigured. In addition, Elijah and Moses suddenly appear. This was a huge moment for these three disciples. After the transfiguration, Jesus brings His disciples back down the mountain. On the way down, Jesus gives them strict instructions not to tell anyone about what had just happened.

When they returned, they saw the other disciples surrounded by a large crowd. The teachers of the law in the crowd were arguing with the disciples. Jesus asked what was being discussed, and a man in the crowd answered His question. He told them that he had brought his demon-possessed son to the disciples and asked them to drive out the evil spirit, but the disciples couldn't do it.

Jesus then said in Mark 9:19, "O unbelieving generation, how long shall I stay with you? How long shall I put up with you? Bring the boy to me."

As usual, Jesus used this situation as a teachable moment for the crowd, as well as for His disciples. Jesus rebuked the evil spirit, and the boy was healed. In their bewilderment and confusion, the disciples pulled Jesus aside in private and asked why they could not do the same thing. Jesus shared a very important lesson with His disciples that we often overlook. Jesus told them that this kind of spirit can only come out by prayer and *fasting*.

Jesus knew that some evil, spiritual strongholds are more powerful than others and require more advanced weaponry. If prayer is a soldier's rifle, then fasting is his rocket launcher. If Jesus was using these terms today, He would say something like this: "This kind of spirit is stronger than most other stubborn, evil spirits. Therefore, soldier, use your rifle, but also use the rocket launcher to blow it up and be done with it."

We have already learned that rocket launchers are tools used by the military to blow things up—in other words, to blow up the enemy's strongholds. Rocket launchers are not used every day. They are bigger and heavier, and their ammo is much bigger. But Jesus would tell us to become trained in how to use our rocket launchers! Don't let them sit and collect dust. Do some damage to the evil principalities that you encounter.

Angela Yuan understood that her son was under demonic influences. She pulled out her megarocket launcher and completed a thirty-nine-day fast on behalf of her son. She got it. She understood strongholds. She made a commitment to *stand in the gap* for her son and say enough is enough! In essence, she was saying, "I will hang on to the hope that I have in Christ Jesus, and I am committed to blowing up this stronghold that has had such a grip on my son." Christopher wasn't able to *stand in the gap* for himself.

He needed help. Help came in the form of a loving mother who was utterly tenacious with her prayer and fasting life.

The result of her thirty-nine-day fast didn't happen overnight. This is a lesson to be learned—we must be patient. I am reminded of the passage in Daniel 10:10–14, where an angel speaks to Daniel. He told Daniel that he was twenty-one days late in delivering a message because the prince of Persia had resisted him. This particular story has always stuck out in my mind whenever I have been praying for something for a long time. We are called to wait and be patient on the Lord. He has His own time-table. However, we are Americans and live in a fast-paced society. We want things done when we want things done. We have been brought up on fast food and thirty-minute sitcoms.

One of the hardest spiritual disciplines (and I do call it a discipline) for me to learn and implement is one word—*wait*! Waiting can be downright painful. When people are in crisis or in pain, the last thing they want to hear is the word *wait*. However, as believers in Christ, we must understand that our Lord works on a different time schedule than ours. He is not lim-ited by the dimension of time.

Warriors or Fat Babies?

What are you going to do? You are coming to the close of this book, and the Holy Spirit is all over you. You are starting to squirm on your fat-baby couch. You know it is coming. You need to take action. You need to make changes in your life. You desire more intimacy with the Lord. The Hound of Heaven is clawing to break in to convict you even further. You are hold-ing it at bay. Are you going to keep your fat-baby diapers, or are you going to man up? There is no end to the trials of life that you are seeing around you. Someone in your sphere of influence needs you to *stand in the gap*, but you have your fat-baby bib on and sit there crying for more milk. If you can't see the need for you to engage in the battle, something is wrong. If there are no trials around you, something is desperately wrong. If nothing else, fast and intercede for this country, which has drifted so far off course in its spiritual direction.

But you say, "I don't know if fasting is for me." Cop-out! "But I don't know how to start." Starting is much like when I learned how to journal for the first time; put the pen to paper and start writing. In other words, just do it. Let me remind you of ten steps to starting your fasting discipline as outlined in chapter 13.

Step One—*Be prayed up.* Ask the Lord for direction as you start your new lifelong discipline of fasting.

Step Two—*Reread Isaiah 58.* This is a key passage to understand as you embark on this new way of life.

Step Three—*Complete the six Bible study lessons on fasting in the appendix of this book.* It is always prudent to further your knowledge of God's principles by digging deeper into His Word. Study by yourself, with a friend, or in your Bible-study group. Whatever you do, dig deeper. The general topic of these studies is Isaiah 58, Pride vs. Humbleness, the Nineveh Fast, the Esther Fast, King Jehoshaphat's Fast, and the Ezra Fast.

Step Four—*Consult your physician.* This is imperative. Seek advice from your healthcare provider.

Step Five—*Start out slowly.* Pick a target day next week—a day where you have no lunch or dinner appointments scheduled. Start small. Commit to fast for two meals that day—maybe fast for breakfast and lunch, and have your evening meal as planned.

Step Six—*Communicate.* Talk to God, talk to your spouse, talk to your doctor, and talk to your family about what the Lord is leading you to do.

Step Seven—*Go to the grocery store.* Go to the store and buy a jug or two of your favorite juice. Experiment! Also be aware that many store-bought juices are packed full of sugar.

Step Eight—*Go to the office-supply store.* Buy a journal. It will become a keepsake for you in the years to come.

Step Nine—*List three prayer requests.* It is imperative that you start correctly. You must have right and pure motives. There must be a spiritual purpose to fast.

Step Ten—*Commit.* Commit to fast one day a week for the next three months.

There you have it: ten steps to launching your fasting discipline. After you have completed one day a week for three months, if the Lord should lead, consider doing a three-day fast. However, never start out with a long, extended fast—*never*! Remember, always consult with your doctor. And always have the right motives.

Jesus is coming back soon! I believe that in my heart of hearts. His return is imminent. All the signs are there. Watch Israel!

Until He returns, there is much work left to be done. Souls need saving. Baby Christians are in need of being discipled. As mature warriors for Christ, we need to rise up and take back the territory which the locusts have eaten. We need spiritual warriors who will fight the good fight (and stay in the fight) with the weapons God has given us—the rifles and rocket launchers of our spiritual weaponry. Learn the tools of the trade of being a warrior. We need more men and women to enlist in the Navy Seals of God's royal army! We need men and women to stand up and say, "Use me, Lord. I will *stand in the gap*!"

Chuck your binkies, and throw away your baby blankets. Now lift your rifles and rocket launchers, take aim, and engage in the spiritual battle!

CHAPTER 19

We Are the Generation of the Frog in the Kettle

A Call to Action

OUR COUNTRY IS in trouble! We have a national debt approaching $20 trillion. Our military is being dismantled before our very eyes. The moral underpinnings have all but been eroded. America is the leader in exporting filth and pornography under the auspices of freedom of speech. We have killed more than fifty-five million babies since *Roe v. Wade* in 1973. Our public schools are a disaster. Our Supreme Court judges are making laws, despite the fact that their jobs are to *rule* on laws, not make them.

Our national sovereignty is being whittled away. Jobs are being shipped overseas. Our immigration policies are in shambles. We are now in a national debate on which bathrooms should be used by whom. Everyone is left to their own devices. The millstone noose is quickly tightening around our necks. The people we elect to public offices to be our voices are at loggerheads with one another and are essentially emasculated. Our way of life and our freedoms are in jeopardy. Down deep we know all of this, but we refuse to take action.

Many of our churches are impotent, producing no fruit. Instead of the Bible shaping our society, society is attempting to shape the Bible. Pastors are leaving the pulpit in droves. Churches were meant to be the launching pads to produce mighty men of God to affect the world for Christ.

Instead, they are producing disciples who have no idea on how to take a public stand for what is right.

Many of our Christian Bible colleges are producing students woefully underprepared for the current societal tsunami. Liberalism has slipped into the fold of professors, and tenure is an outdated form of cronyism.

We are that generation—*we are the generation of the frog in the kettle.* We may have just crossed the point of no return for the United States of America. Is the hand of God's judgment near, or has it already arrived? Can we correlate the national disasters at hand—the floods, tornados, and wildfires—to the mighty hand of God trying desperately to grab our attention? We have taken prayer and God out of our schools. We have taken the Ten Commandments off of public property. Yet we are dismayed when such national disasters occur and have the immaturity to ask, "Why, God?"

Whatever the answer is, we need a believer who understands the power of fasting, who has a national platform, and who has national clout to call for a "Day of Fasting, Humiliation, and Prayer before a Holy and Righteous God," much like our Founding Fathers did many years ago. It is one thing to call for a season of fasting in *word*, but it is a totally separate issue to call a nation to turn from its evil ways and repent of its sins in *action*, much like the king of Nineveh did in the times of Jonah.

It all starts with the church. In Philippians 4:17, the Bible states, "For it is time for the judgment to begin with the family of God." If the church does not step up, how can we expect the unbelieving world to step up. The question is posed, will we have the courage under extreme persecution to turn from our evil ways? As a nation we must never forget from whence we came and above all never forget the promises of God and His Holy Word, much like we find in 2 Chronicles 7:14:

> If my people, who are called by my name,
> Will humble themselves and pray and seek my face
> And turn from their wicked ways,
> Then will I hear from heaven
> And will forgive their sin and will heal their land.

194

Appendix

About Prisoners For Christ
Outreach Ministries

Prisoners For Christ Outreach Ministries (PFC) is a ministry dedicated to taking the Gospel of Jesus Christ into the jails, prisons, and juvenile institutions of the world. At this writing, PFC and its army of over one thousand volunteers worldwide conducted over 5,800 church services and Bible studies in 2015. That is an average of more than fifteen services per day. With that, over a million inmates were in attendance, and over two hundred thousand accepted Christ for the first time.

Originally started in the state of Washington, PFC has centers of influence in thirteen different countries, including Russia, Nepal, India, Kenya, Uganda, Rwanda, Burundi, the Congo, Malawi, Ghana, Togo, Burkina Faso, and the Philippines, with more than ten additional countries waiting to come online. In addition, PFC has a two-year Bible study correspondence course and a pen pal program, as well as our national inmate newspaper, *Yard Out*, for inmates here in the United States. We exist for the sole purpose of sharing the love of Christ to the lost in the prisons of the world.

1. If you have a loved one in prison and would like some Christian literature sent to that person, please go online at www.prisonersforchrist.org to submit a literature request.
2. If you would like to receive our current annual report, either in print or electronically, please go to the website and request a copy.

3. If you would like to volunteer or develop a PFC outpost in your state, please go to the website and request our franchise brochure.
4. If you would like to make a donation to PFC, please go to the website, and at the bottom of the page, click *Give*.

Government Officials Who Have Called for Fasting

In the following pages of the appendix, I have printed excerpts from various statements and proclamations made by federal government officials who have stepped forward throughout our history to declare days of *fasting, humiliation, and prayer* for a once-great nation. We need Christian mayors, governors, senior pastors, and Bible college presidents to take a stand and have a call for a solemn day of fasting (with true repentance in our hearts), which will ultimately lead to true revival in our land. These excerpts are provided as originally written.

The Assembly of Virginia: June 1, 1774

Tuesday, the 24th of May, King George III, 1774. This House, being deeply impressed with the Apprehension of the *great Dangers*, to be derived to British America, from the hostile Invasion of the City of Boston, in our Sister Colony of Massachusetts Bay,...deem it highly necessary that the said first Day of June to be set apart by the Members of this House as a Day of *Fasting, Humiliation, and Prayer*, devoutly to implore the divine Interposition, for averting the heavy Calamity which threatens Destruction to our civil Rights.[61] (Emphasis added.)

Massachusetts Provincial Congress: April 15, 1775 (Four Days before the Battle of Lexington)

In circumstances dark as these, it becomes us, as men and Christians, to reflect that, whilst every prudent measure should be taken to ward off the impending judgments...the 11th of May next be set apart as a *Day of Public Humiliation, Fasting and Prayer*...to confess the sins...to implore the Forgiveness of all our Transgression.[62] (Emphasis added.)

President John Adams: July 12, 1775

President John Adams wrote a letter to his wife explaining the Continental Congress's decision to declare a Day of Public Humiliation, Fasting, and Prayer:

We have appointed a Continental fast. *Millions will be upon their knees at once before their great Creator*, imploring His forgiveness and blessing; His smiles on American Council and arms.[63] (Emphasis added.)

Continental Congress: March 16, 1776

In times of *impending calamity and distress*; when the liberties of America are imminently endangered by the secret machinations and open assaults of an insidious and vindictive administration, it becomes the indispensable duty of these hitherto free and happy colonies, with true penitence of heart, and the most reverent devotion, publickly to acknowledge the *over ruling providence of God*; to confess and deplore our offences against him; and to supplicate his interposition for averting the threatened danger, and prospering our strenuous efforts in the cause of freedom, virtue, and posterity.

...Desirous, at the same time, to have people of all ranks and degrees duly impressed with a solemn sense of God's superintending providence, and of their duty, devoutly to rely, in all their lawful enterprizes, on his aid and direction, Do earnestly recommend, that Friday, the Seventeenth day of May next, be observed by the said colonies as a day *of humiliation, fasting, and prayer*; that we may, with united hearts, confess and bewail our manifold sins and transgressions, and, by a sincere repentance and amendment of life, appease his righteous displeasure, and, *through the merits and mediation of Jesus Christ*, obtain his pardon and forgiveness; *humbly imploring his assistance to frustrate the cruel purposes of our unnatural enemies*;

...that it may please the Lord of Hosts, the God of Armies, to animate our officers and soldiers with invincible fortitude, to guard and protect them in the day of battle, and to crown the continental arms, by sea and land, with victory and success: Earnestly beseeching him to bless our civil rulers, and the representatives of the people, in their several assemblies and conventions; to preserve and strengthen their union, to inspire them with an ardent, disinterested love of their country; to give wisdom and stability to their counsels; and direct them to the most efficacious measures for establishing the rights of America on the most honourable and permanent basis—That he would be graciously pleased to bless all his people in these colonies with health and plenty, and *grant that a spirit of incorruptible patriotism*, and of pure undefiled religion, may universally prevail; and this continent be speedily restored to the blessings of peace and liberty, and enabled to transmit them inviolate to the latest posterity. And it is recommended to Christians of all denominations, to assemble for public worship, and abstain from servile labour on the said day. [64] (Emphasis added.)

Massachusetts Governor Samuel Adams: February 28, 1795
A Proclamation for a Day of PUBLIC FASTING, HUMILIATION and PRAYER:

THE supreme Ruler of the Universe, having been pleased, in the course of his Providence, to establish the Independence of the United States of America, and to cause them to assume their rank, amount the nations of the Earth, and bless them with Liberty, Peace and Plenty; we ought to be led by Religious feelings of Gratitude; *and to walk before Him, in all Humility, according to his most Holy Law*. But, as the depravity of our Hearts has, in so many instances drawn us aside from the path of duty, so that we have frequently offended our Divine and Merciful Benefactor; it is therefore highly incumbent on us, according to the ancient and laudable practice of our pious Ancestors, *to open the year by a public and solemn Fast*. That with true repentance and contrition of Heart, we may unitedly implore the forgiveness of our Sins, *through the merits of Jesus Christ*, and humbly supplicate our Heavenly Father, to grant us the aids of his Grace, for the amendment of our Hearts and Lives, and vouchsafe his smiles upon our temporal concerns:

I HAVE therefore thought fit to appoint, and with the advice and consent of the Council, I do hereby appoint Thursday, the Second Day of April next, to be observed as a Day of Public *Fasting, Humiliation and Prayer* throughout this Commonwealth: Calling upon the Ministers of the Gospel, of every Denomination, with their respective Congregations, to assemble on that Day, and devoutly implore the Divine forgiveness of our Sins, *To pray that the Light of the Gospel, and the rights of Conscience,* may be continued to the people of United America; and that his Holy Word may be improved by them, so that the *name of God may be exalted,* and their own Liberty and Happiness secured. That he would be graciously pleased to bless our Federal Government; that by a wise administration, it may be a sure guide and safe protection in national concerns, for the people who have established, and who support it. That He would continue to us the invaluable Blessings of Civil Liberty; guarding us against intestine commotions; and enabling the United States, in the exercise of such Governmental powers, as are devolved upon them, so that the honor and dignity of our Nation, upon the Sea and the Land, may be supported, and Peace with the other Powers of the World, upon safe and honorable terms, may be maintained. [65] (Emphasis added.)

President John Adams: March 6, 1799

For these reasons I have thought proper to recommend, and I do hereby recommend accordingly, that Thursday, the 25th day of April next, be observed throughout the United States of America as a day of *solemn humiliation, fasting, and prayer*; that the citizens on that day abstain as far as may be from their secular occupations, devote the time to the sacred duties of religion in public and in private; that they call to mind our numerous offenses against the Most High God, confess them before Him with the sincerest penitence, *implore His pardoning mercy, through the Great Mediator and Redeemer, for our past transgressions, and that through the grace of His Holy Spirit* we may be disposed and enabled to yield a more suitable obedience to His righteous requisitions in time to come; that He would interpose to arrest the progress of that impiety and licentiousness in principle and practice so offensive to Himself and so ruinous to mankind; that He would make us deeply sensible that "righteousness exalteth a nation, but sin is a reproach to any people;" that He would turn us from our transgressions and turn His displeasure from us; that He would withhold us from unreasonable discontent, from disunion, faction, sedition, and insurrection; that He would preserve our country from the desolating sword; that He would save our cities and towns from a repetition of those awful pestilential visitations under which they have lately suffered so severely, and that the health of our inhabitants generally may be precious in His sight; that *He would favor us with fruitful seasons and so bless the labors of the husbandman as that there may be food in abundance for man and beast; that He would prosper our commerce, manufactures, and fisheries, and give success to the people in all their lawful industry and enterprise; that He would smile on our colleges, academies, schools, and seminaries of learning, and make them nurseries of sound science, morals, and religion; that He would bless all magistrates, from the highest to the lowest, give them the true spirit of their station, make them a terror to evil doers and a praise to them that do well; that He would preside over the councils of the nation at this critical period, enlighten them to a just discernment of the public interest, and save them from mistake, division, and discord; that He would make succeed our preparations for defense and bless our armaments by land and by sea; that He would put an end to the effusion of human blood and the accumulation of human misery among the contending nations of the earth by disposing them to justice, to equity, to benevolence, and to peace; and that he would extend the blessings of knowledge, of true liberty, and of pure and undefiled religion throughout the world.* [66] (Emphasis added.)

CONNECTICUT GOVERNOR JONATHAN TRUMBULL: 1807

WHEN we seriously consider the Being and Perfections of God, with our relation to and dependence on Him, as our Great Creator, Preserver and

Benefactor; and when we reflect on the Evil of our Ways, and the folly of our Conduct toward the Author of our Being and of all our Mercies, *we should be humbled in the Dust before our God, for our sinful Ingratitude and unworthiness*: We have reason to cry out with the humble Publican, "*God be merciful to us Sinners.*"

WITH these Impressions I have thought proper to appoint, and I do hereby appoint Friday the Twenty-Seventh Day of March next, to be observed as a Day of *Fasting*, Humiliation and Prayer throughout this State. And I do hereby call upon the People of all denominations of Religion, devoutly and solemnly to keep said Day and appropriate it as a Day of special religious service, devoted to God in solemn Duties of penitential acknowledgment of their Sins, private and social, against the Divine Will and government: and while lamenting their Sins, and forming sincere and humble resolutions of new Obedience, may they be solicitous to keep the Day in such manner as may be acceptable to God, and prove of lasting benefit in their future Lives and Conduct. At the same time it will become us humbly to reflect upon and seriously to consider the Judgments of the Lord, which in various ways, at this time, seem peculiarly abroad in the Earth; and endeavor to search out the procuring causes of God's singular Displeasure. "*When the Lord ariseth to shake terribly the Earth,*" *may the People return to their God. "It may be we shall be hid in the Day of the Lord's fierce anger.*" [67] (Emphasis added.)

Massachusetts Governor Christopher Gore: April 15, 1810

In conformity with the invariable usage of the commonwealth, and with a sense of our absolute dependence on the beneficent parent of mankind, and of our numerous and *aggravated offenses against his holy will and commandments*, I have thought fit to appoint, and by and with the advice and consent of the council, I do appoint THURSDAY, the FIFTH DAY of APRIL next, as a Day of *Public Humiliation, Fasting, and Prayer in this Commonwealth*. And I do request the Ministers and People of every denomination throughout the same, to assemble on that day, in their several places of Public Worship, that we may unitedly humble ourselves in the presence of Almighty God, and acknowledge with deep contrition, our manifold sins and transgressions; that we may devoutly deprecate his judgments, and implore His merciful forgiveness, through the merits of our blessed Lord and Redeemer. [68]

President James Madison: November 25, 1814

The two Houses of the National Legislature having by a joint resolution expressed their desire that in the present time of public calamity and war a day may be recommended to be observed by the people of the United States as a day of *public humiliation and fasting and of prayer to Almighty God for the safety and welfare of these States*, His blessing on their arms, and a speedy restoration of peace, I have deemed it proper by this proclamation to recommend that Thursday, the 12th of January next, be set apart as a day on which all may have an opportunity of voluntarily offering at the same time in their respective religious assemblies their humble adoration to the Great Sovereign of the Universe, of confessing their sins and transgressions, and of strengthening their vows of repentance and amendment. They will be invited by the same solemn occasion to call to mind the distinguished favors conferred on the American people in the general health which has been enjoyed, in the abundant fruits of the season, in the progress of the arts instrumental to their comfort, their prosperity, and their security, and in the victories which have so powerfully contributed to the defense and protection of our country, a devout thankfulness for all which ought to be mingled with their supplications to the Beneficent Parent of the Human Race *that He would be graciously pleased to pardon all their offenses against Him*; to support and animate them in the discharge of their respective duties; to continue to them the precious advantages flowing from political institutions so auspicious to their safety against dangers from abroad, to their tranquility at home, and to their liberties, civil and religious; and that He would in a special manner preside over the nation in its public councils and constituted authorities, giving wisdom to its measures and success to its arms in maintaining its rights and in overcoming all hostile designs and attempts against it; and, finally, that by inspiring the enemy with dispositions favorable to a just and reasonable peace its blessings may be speedily and happily restored. [69] (Emphasis added.)

PRESIDENT JAMES BUCHANAN: DECEMBER 14, 1860
Numerous appeals have been made to me by pious and patriotic associations and citizens, in view of the present distracted and dangerous condition of our country, to recommend that a day be set apart for Humiliation, *Fasting* and Prayer throughout the Union.

In compliance with their request and my own sense of duty, I designate Friday, the 4th of January 1861, for this purpose, and recommend that the People assemble on that day, according to their several forms of worship, to keep it as a *solemn Fast.*

The Union of the States is at the present moment *threatened with alarming and immediate danger; panic and distress* of a fearful character prevails throughout the land; our laboring population are without employment, and consequently deprived of the means of earning their bread. Indeed, hope seems to have deserted the minds of men. *All classes are in a state of confusion and dismay*, and the wisest counsels of our best and purest men are wholly disregarded. (Emphasis added.)

In this the hour of our calamity and peril, to whom shall we resort for relief but to the God of our fathers? His omnipotent arm only can save us from the awful effects of our own crimes and follies——our own ingratitude and guilt toward our Heavenly Father.

Let us, then, with deep contrition and penitent sorrow, *unite in humbling ourselves* before the Most High, in confessing our individual and national sins, and in acknowledging the injustice of our punishment. Let us implore Him to remove from our hearts that false pride of opinion which would impel us to persevere in wrong for the sake of consistency, rather than yield a just submission to the unforeseen exigencies by which we are now surrounded. Let us with deep reverence beseech him to restore the friendship and good will which prevailed in former days among the people of the several States; and, above all, to save us from the horrors of civil war and "blood-guiltiness." Let our fervent prayers ascend to His Throne that He would not desert us in this hour of extreme peril, but remember us as he did our fathers in the darkest days of the revolution; and preserve our Constitution and our Union, the work of their hands, for ages yet to come. [70] (Emphasis added.)

PRESIDENT ABRAHAM LINCOLN: MARCH 30, 1863 (PROCLAIMED THREE FASTS)

...And whereas it is the duty of nations as well as of men, to own their dependence upon the overruling power of God, to confess their sins and transgressions, in humble sorrow, yet with assured hope that genuine repentance will lead to mercy and pardon; *and to recognize the sublime truth, announced in the Holy Scriptures and proven by all history, that those nations only are blessed whose God is the Lord.*

And, insomuch as we know that, by His divine law, nations like individuals are subjected to punishments and chastisements in this world, may we not justly fear that the awful calamity of civil war, which now desolates the land, may be but a punishment, inflicted upon us, for our presumptuous sins, to the needful end of our national reformation as a whole People? We have been the *recipients of the choicest bounties of Heaven.* We have been preserved, these many years, in peace and prosperity. *We have grown in numbers, wealth and power, as no other nation has ever grown. But we have forgotten God. We have forgotten the gracious hand which preserved us in peace, and multiplied and enriched and strengthened us; and we have vainly imagined, in the deceitfulness of our hearts, that all these blessings were produced by some superior wisdom and virtue of our own. Intoxicated with unbroken success, we have become too self-sufficient to feel the necessity of redeeming and preserving grace, too proud to pray to the God that made us!*

It behooves us then, to humble ourselves before the offended Power, to confess our national sins, and to pray for clemency and forgiveness. [71](Emphasis added.)

From 1863 to 2011: A period of silence from Government officials until just recently!

TEXAS GOVERNOR RICK PERRY: MAY 23, 2011

In 1775, the Continental Congress asked the colonies to join in prayer, seeking wisdom as they faced the responsibility and opportunity of building a new nation. As leaders of that young nation assembled in 1787 to craft a Constitution, Benjamin Franklin implored the framers to pray for guidance, famously declaring, "The longer I live, the more convincing proofs I see of this truth: that God governs in the affairs of men." Decades later, during a time of national turmoil, President John Adams declared "a day of solemn humiliation, fasting and prayer," asking citizens of all faiths to pray for America's protection from danger. Later, as civil war tore our young country apart, President Abraham Lincoln proclaimed a day of national fasting and prayer, saying "It behooves us…to humble ourselves before the offended Power, to confess our national sins, and to pray to the God that made us." During World War II, with our troops locked in battle on the beaches of France, President Franklin D. Roosevelt led the nation in prayer, "As we rise to each new day, and again when each day is spent, let words of prayer be on our lips, invoking Thy help to our efforts."

Given the trials that have beset our country and world—from the global economic downturn to natural disasters, the lingering danger of terrorism and wars that endanger our troops in Iraq, Afghanistan and theaters of conflict around the globe, and the decline of our culture in the context of the demise of families—it seems imperative that the people of our nation should once again join together for a solemn day of prayer and *fasting* on behalf of our troubled nation.

In times of trouble, even those who have been granted power by the people must turn to God in humility for wisdom, mercy and direction. In the spirit of the *Book of Joel, chapter 2, Verses 15–16*, I urge a solemn gathering of prayer and *fasting*. As those verses admonish: *"15 Blow the trumpet in Zion, declare a holy fast, call a sacred assembly...16 Gather the people, consecrate the assembly..." As Jesus prayed publicly for the benefit of others in John 11:41–42, so should we express our faith in this way.*

THEREFORE, I invite my fellow Texans to join me on August 6 at Reliant Stadium in Houston, as we pray for unity and righteousness—for this great state, this great nation and all mankind. I urge Americans of faith to pray on that day for the healing of our country, the rebuilding of our communities and the restoration of enduring values as our guiding force.[72](Emphasis added.)

Louisiana Governor Bobby Jindal: January 23, 2015 (Prayer Event)

As our nation faces unprecedented crises—culturally, socially, and financially—'The Response Louisiana' is a call for worshippers in Louisiana and around the country to come together in unity for prayer and *fasting*. This event has one purpose and one purpose only: *To approach God in humility* and pray for his mercy, grace and guidance for our nation, which has *lost its moral foundation and is suffering from a crisis of faith.*

It's so encouraging to see Christians from across denominational and cultural backgrounds join in this time of prayer, and we truly believe God will be faithful to His Word. [73](Emphasis added.)

A Special Note to Parents of Inmates

(Prodigal Sons or Daughters in Prison or Jail)

I OFTENTIMES COUNSEL heartbroken parents over the phone when their prodigal son or daughter has landed in jail time and time again. Usually these prodigals are demanding that their parents bail them out. It is hard for me to say, and it is hard for the parents to hear, but 99 percent of the time, I counsel parents *not* to bail their kids out of jail. Doing this will only enable them to continue in their destructive lifestyle on the outside. They want one thing and one thing only: to be released from jail so they can continue down their path of destruction, addiction, and poor choices. They will say and do anything to manipulate their parents.

Too many times I have seen men, women, and children, who may have no other way to come to know the Lord except by spending time in jail or prison, suddenly be bailed out by well-meaning parents or friends. I have heard hundreds of testimonies from inmates who have stood up in church services in jails and prisons to praise the Lord for sending them to jail because, otherwise, they would have been dead by now. Parents don't have the luxury of hearing those testimonies. When you say no to bailing out your prodigals, be prepared for the shouting and cursing to begin. They are not going to like you. They will say some pretty hurtful things. However, do not bend. Know that it is the enemy speaking through your adult children. You didn't put them there; they put themselves there.

Think of jails and prisons two different ways: *first* as an emergency room of a hospital, and *second* as a university.

Emergency rooms are where very sick people in need of immediate medical care go to obtain treatment. There are only four possible outcomes for people who enter an emergency room.

1. They find help, are treated, and are quickly released.
2. They find help, they stay longer than they had expected, they recover, and they are released.
3. They attempt to find help, but they are released sicker than when they came in.
4. They attempt to find help, but because their condition is terminal, they die in the hospital.

These are the exact same outcomes for people who enter jail and prison. There are no other options. If an inmate will be quiet and listen to that still, small voice, his or her life could be changed forever. It is happening all around the world by the hundreds of thousands. Inmates are hearing that still, small voice and starting to put their lives back together by accepting Jesus as their Lord and Savior.

The *second* way to think of a jail or prison is to think of it as a university, or should I say the School of Hard Knocks.

1. Some people graduate with honors from this school; they have a true life-change and go on to a better life.
2. Some float through school doing the minimum to graduate. They don't attempt to change and are no different from when they entered.
3. Others flunk out and do it over. Those who flunk out of school are those who don't get it. Sometimes they have to enroll and reenroll and reenroll in the School of Hard Knocks until they do get it. Some never get it! This is the inmate who keeps the revolving doors of prisons in business: in and out, in and out, and in and out.

Ninety-nine percent of the time I suggest to parents that they leave their prodigals right where they are. You don't want to block what God is about to do in their lives while they are incarcerated. For the most part, they are probably safer in jail than they are out on the streets, where they are wallowing in their addictions.

One percent of the time I tell parents to go rescue their kid. This is when a good kid makes a dumb mistake and is in the wrong place at the wrong time. A good kid is defined as being respectful of his parents, succeeding in school, and progressing in knowing Jesus, and this is his first arrest—not his third or fourth. At this stage it is *not* important that he go through the trials of jail time. Go get him. Have a teachable moment. Love on him and tell him you won't come for him a second time.

However, if you have a good kid, but all of sudden you observe that he is hanging out with some really bad characters, then you may consider leaving your child in jail for a couple of extra days for the reality check of life to sink in. Friends of your children are like the proverbial canaries in the mine. Parents, keep watching the canaries (your kids' friends) to see that they remain healthy. If they are not, this can be a big red flag for your own child's well-being and safety.

If your child has a life-threatening medical condition and is not being treated properly, I would encourage you to call the institution immediately and inform the staff of the situation. In most circumstances, if your child is found guilty of the alleged crimes, he will either do his sentence at the local jail (if the sentence is less than one year) or at a state prison (if the sentence is longer than a year). Regardless, you as the parent—as well as your incarcerated child—should use this incarceration period as a time to draw close to the Lord.

There are many Bible-based prison ministries around the country that have Bible study correspondence courses, pen pal programs, in-prison Bible studies, or visitation programs. Do some research and find out what prison ministries are in your local area. Instruct your prodigal to check out the chaplaincy program at the institution. Use this time to disciple your child through the mail, or better yet, have someone from your church become involved with him through a letter-writing campaign. There are many people sitting in the pews of our churches who are just waiting to be asked to serve the Lord in some capacity.

Feel free to check out Prisoners For Christ Outreach Ministries' website at www.prisonersforchrist.org for further resources.

A Six-Week Small-Group Bible Study

———— § ————

Understanding Isaiah 58

Introduction

To UNDERSTAND GOD's heartbeat toward fasting, one doesn't have to go any farther than Isaiah 58. This is a complete chapter on God's design and desire for His children when it comes to fasting. We read that the nation of Israel was grumbling because they were going through the work of fasting but were not seeing any results. They were like little kindergartners. They were whining about not having their prayers answered. God reveals to them their weaknesses and admonishes them for failing to adopt a lifetime of God-honoring fasting. In this chapter, God reveals to His children the areas He holds in high regard and what the results would be if one adopted this lifestyle. Read Isaiah chapter 58.

1. Explain what is happening in verse 2. Does this sound like America? Why or why not?

2. In the first half of verse 3, the nation is whining about their circumstances. Why? In essence, what are they saying to God?

3. What is God's response in verses 3b–4?

4. What are the four areas God lists as wrong with their fasting in 3b–4a? Have you ever struggled with any of those four areas in your life? Please feel free to share with the group. What did you do to attempt to overcome those areas of weakness?

5. God makes a bold statement in verse 4b. What is it, and what is He saying?

6. In verses 6–7 God actually lists eight things that He is looking for in their fasting.
   a. List those eight items.
   b. Which are the things you are good at?
   c. What areas need improvement in your life?
7. In verses 8–11, God provides a list of twelve items that are promises if we will fast according to His guidelines.
   a. List those twelve items.
   b. Name three areas that you most desire in your life from this list. Explain why you desire those items.

——— § ———

Understanding Pride vs. Humbleness

Introduction

STUART SCOTT, IN his book *From Pride to Humility*, says, "When someone is proud he or she is focused on self. This is a form of self-worship. Prideful people believe that they are or should be the *source* of what is good, right and worthy of praise...In essence, they are believing that all things should be *from* them, *through* them, and *to* them or *for* them. Pride is competitive toward others, and especially toward God. Pride wants to be on top. Thomas Watson is quoted to have said, 'Pride seeks to ungod God.' This phrase certainly describes the arrogant." [74]

1. Read Luke 14:11. Explain in your own words what this verse says to you. Explain to the group a time in your life when you lived by the exact opposite of this command.

2. What was the outcome of your life situation during this season of life? Was it painful? How did you realize that this was not the biblical way to live your life?

3. Did a family member or friend confront you on your pride? How did you react when they confronted you on this manner of living?

4. Since that time, how have you changed? What caused you to change? Do you have more changing that needs to occur?

5. Read Psalm 18:27, Psalm 25:9, Psalm 149:4, and Proverbs 3:34. How does the Lord feel about humble people?

6. How humble of a person are you? On a scale of 1–10, with 10 being the most humble, how high do you rate yourself on the humbleness scale? What changes need to happen for you to be better in this area of humbleness?

7. Ask your spouse to rate you in this area. Ask a best friend to rate you in this area. How do you think they will rate you? Will it be significantly different than how you rate yourself?

8. Read Psalm 31:23, Psalm 101:5, Psalm 138:6, Proverbs 16:5, and Proverbs 21:4.

   a. How does the Lord feel toward those who are prideful?

   b. How does this make you feel about being prideful?

   c. What are you going to do to make changes in your life not to be so prideful?

9. The Bible says that we are to be "imitators of God." If that is the case, what do you need to do to move in that direction?

10. How would you counsel a young person or couple in their midtwenties regarding pride and humility?

11. What three things did the Holy Spirit reveal to you by completing this lesson?

Understanding Jonah and the Ninevites Fast

Introduction

ISRAEL WAS IN full rebellion against God because of their stubborn hearts and their practice of idolatry. Throughout the Old Testament, the Lord would always chastise Israel for their sins. He oftentimes would do this in the form of an army coming against His chosen people and taking them captive.

God sent an army from the north around 775 BC. They were called the Assyrians. The Assyrians were a brutal and ruthless people. They were an evil empire. They committed many atrocities and war crimes against their enemies. Just the name *Assyria* struck a chord of fear among the Israelite nation. The Assyrians were a much-hated and dreaded enemy of Israel. Anyone growing up in this era would have been very familiar with the atrocities of the Assyrian nation, much the same way we are very familiar with the atrocities perpetrated by the Islamic group ISIS. Nineveh was the capital of Assyria.

Many people think that Jonah is a story about a big fish. It is actually a story of a whole lot more. Let's pick up the story in Jonah chapter 3.

1. Read chapter 3. In verses 2 and 3, the Bible makes some claims about the city of Nineveh. In verse 2 the Bible describes Nineveh as a great city, and in verse 3 it is described as a very important city, requiring three days to go through it. Why do you think Nineveh is described this way?

2. When Jonah arrived, he had a message to proclaim. What was that message (verse 4)?

3. It was a simple message—in fact it was a message of only eight words. How can this simple principle of brevity relate to us in this very complicated world?

4. In verse 5 the Bible says the Ninevites believed God. How can this happen with such a simple message?

5. In verse 5 the Bible also says they declared a fast.

   a. How did this wicked city know anything about fasting?

   b. Does it say just a few fasted or maybe just the religious fasted?

   c. Who fasted in verse 5?

6. In verse 6 this story goes to a whole new level. It is one thing for the commoner to understand the message, but in verse 6 it says the king ordered a proclamation that every man and beast should fast. Why did he do this?

7. What would America be like if our political leaders called a fast before any major decision?

   a. Do you think that could ever be possible?

   b. Did our leaders call a fast after 9/11?

   c. Do you remember any of our leaders calling a fast before any major military conflict?

8. What was God's outcome to this humbleness?

9. List the last three major trials for your family. Did you call a fast? Why or why not? What will you do the next time?

10. If you are a business owner, list the last three major trials of your business. Did you call a fast? Why or why not? What will you do the next time?

11. If you are a head of your family, leader in your business or church, or even your own Christian ministry, what would prevent you from calling for a fast? What must happen in order for you to overcome this pride?

12. What three things did the Holy Spirit reveal to you by completing this lesson?

Understanding Esther's Fast

Introduction

THE BOOK OF Esther, like the book of Jonah, is another great book of God's faithfulness and compassion for His chosen people. Much like the book of Jonah, where the Ninevites were about to face certain death by the hands of God, in the book of Esther, the Jews were about ready to face certain death by the hands of the ungodly. This story line is all about a life-and-death struggle—what man did to prevent it and what God ends up doing.

Esther was a faithful Jewish woman who knew what she had to do. She knew the only solution to the crisis was to approach the king. She also knew the law of the land—if you approach the king without an invite and it displeases the king, this could mean certain death. By reading Esther 4:15–16, we can surmise that Esther was actually fearing for her life. But not appealing to the king would mean certain death for many Jews. Mordecai and Esther were between a rock and hard place.

1. Read 3:8–11. Evil has taken root. A plan has been hatched out of the vileness of Haman's heart. What just happened? Why did this happen?

2. In 3:10 what is the significance of the king giving Haman his signet ring?

    a. Read 4:1–2. What was Mordecai's response?

    b. What did he wear? What was the significance of that?

3. In all of the far provinces, what did the Jews do (verse 3)? Did they fast? Why did they fast?

4. Mordecai knew what needed to be done (verse 8). Esther must make an appeal to the king. Reread verses 9–11. Why was Mordecai receiving pushback from Esther?

5. Mordecai offers up his most famous quote in verse 14: "And who knows but that you have come to a royal position for such a time as this." Many Christians are in prominent positions in the government and in their businesses. Why do some Christians fail to realize that God has positioned them for such a time as this? What do you think are their fears?

6. Esther's life is at stake. She offers up a partnership solution in 4:15. What is it?

7. How long of a fast is she recommending? Is it just from food? The body can go without food for many days, but it cannot go without water for more than a few days. Why do you think she is calling for such a drastic fast?

8. Fasting breaks through to the heavenlies. By fasting we may *not* see the results we are looking for in the short term, but we do find peace from on high. What are Esther's lasts words in verse 15? Do you think she has found peace?

9. What trials are you going through right now? Do you need to fast over these trials?

10. What three things did the Holy Spirit reveal to you by completing this lesson?

§

Understanding King Jehoshaphat's Fast

Introduction

KING JEHOSHAPHAT REIGNED around 873–849 BC. We learn in earlier passages that King Jehoshaphat was a good king who, in his early years, was fully devoted to the Lord. However, he was not without fault, as he had made three disastrous alliances during his reign. But in 2 Chronicles 20, we pick up the story in verses 1–3, where his advisors come to him and tell him that a vast army is coming against him and the nation.

1. Read 2 Chronicles 20:1–2. What was the urgency?
2. What did this mean for the king and his people?
3. The Bible uses four key words in verse 3: alarmed, resolved, inquire, and fast. Why was the king alarmed? What is the definition of resolve? What is the definition of inquire?
4. Why did he call a fast?
5. In verse 4 the Bible says, "The people of Judah came together to seek help from the Lord." When was the last time you heard the leaders of America seeking help from the Lord? Has our prosperity and military might caused us to look elsewhere for our help? What is the danger in doing that? What can be done to turn that around?
6. Reread 20:12. King Jehoshaphat makes three statements in this verse. What are those three statements, and what does that tell you about the severity of the problem?

7. When he says, "We do not know what to do," it gives us a clue as to his ability to make decisions. He is in dire straits. His people were looking toward him for solutions. Then he says, "our eyes are on you." This is a peek into his heart. What do you think was going on in his heart, mind, and soul?

8. Reread 20:15–18. A man by the name of Jahaziel stands up in the assembly and makes some pretty bold statements. What were those bold statements? What can we learn from these verses when we go through trials?

9. In verse 17 he says, "You will not have to fight this battle." What would you think if you heard somebody say this to you in a life-and-death situation? Would you believe him?

10. How does 2 Chronicles 20:17 relate or compare to Isaiah 58:8?

11. What was the outcome of this battle in verse 24? What encouragement does that give you as you walk through your personal trials?

12. What three things did the Holy Spirit reveal to you by completing this lesson?

—— § ——

Understanding Ezra's Fast

Introduction

EZRA WAS CALLED on a mission to go back to Jerusalem. The trip was approximately nine hundred miles and would take Ezra and his companions several months to complete. In addition, the road back to Jerusalem would take them through rough terrain with many bandits on the way. Ezra knew what he was up against. Besides that, he was taking back a boatload of cash. He was concerned for loss of life as well as loss of property. He did not want to tell the king that he needed a military escort. He was in need of divine intervention, so he called a fast. He and his people humbled themselves by the river to call upon God's favor for traveling mercies.

Ezra needed to make physical as well as spiritual preparations. Many times, we as believers shoot up quick and glib prayers. However, the most serious situations need prayer concentration in conjunction with fasting.

1. Read Ezra 8:21–23. What did Ezra do in verse 21? Why?
2. Why was he so concerned for the safety of his family and friends?
3. How much money was he taking along with him? Read 8:26–27. Some believe he was carrying upward of twenty-five tons of silver, or approximately $20 million. Now answer the question: Why was he so concerned?
4. Ezra knew what he was up against. He gathered his people and called a fast so that they might have a safe journey. Have you ever been on a short-term mission trip? Did you fast for a safe journey? Why or why not?

5. Some say the world is more evil today than it was back then. If that is the case, then why don't more mission-trip leaders call for a season of fasting before embarking on their trips?

6. Reread verse 22. Why was Ezra ashamed to tell the king? Isn't being ashamed (of being forthright) a form of pride?

7. What was the outcome of their prayers and fasting? Read verses 31–32. What can we glean from this story of Ezra?

8. One of the biblical examples of fasting is when the leadership of an organization or government calls for a fast. How will you encourage the leadership of your next short-term mission trip to fast? What will you say, and how will you convey that message?

9. When was the last time someone in the leadership of the American government called for a fast? When was the last time you heard a megachurch pastor calling for a fast for America or the nation of Israel? What should be your role?

10. What are the things that are ravaging this great country? If God did call you to fast for this country, what would be your specific prayer requests during your fast?

11. Would you invite someone to partner with you in the fast? Make a list of three people you would like to invite to fast.

12. What three things did the Holy Spirit reveal to you by completing this lesson?

Journal Entries from the Second Fast

SUNDAY, FEBRUARY 24, 2002—DAY EIGHT OF THE FAST

EIGHT DAYS INTO the fast. It is not getting any easier, and it seems as if it is harder than the very first fast. However, I am so proud of my wife. It seems as if the Lord is doing an incredible work in her. I am really blessed by denying myself any food. The body and mind are weak; it is only through the all-sufficiency of the Lord and the empowerment of the Holy Spirit that sustains me. I am waiting for the spiritual eyes of the last fast. I wait with incredible expectation of the fast.

SUNDAY MARCH 24, 2002—DAY THIRTY-SIX OF THE FAST

Back home from vacation down in Florida. I have been tempted more these past five days than any other time of this fast or the previous fast. I feel I have to fight 1,000 percent more just to sustain and not collapse by grabbing a piece of pizza. Denying myself of the world's best foods has been incredibly hard. Lord, you have clearly prodded me in prayer and discipline. Outside of my first trip to India, this is the most I have ever journaled.

You have given me great prayers and visions for the future. You have empowered me to memorize scripture. All these are incredible blessings of this fast. I would not give up any portion of these blessings in order to relieve the pain. You have granted me incredible clarity of mind and an incredible amount of effectiveness, but oh, it seems so hard, much harder than before. Father, sustain me; don't let me fail being so close.

TUESDAY MARCH 26, 2002—DAY THIRTY-EIGHT OF THE FAST
Today I awake with a sense of dread, fear, and anxiety. Something unlike I have ever experienced on this fast before. It was a fear of health-related issues. The enemy caused a full-frontal attack on my entire being. I had doubts of self-worth, insecurities, and fears about this fast. Was I doing this fast out of my own strength?

I sinned by not immediately rebuking this spirit of dread that was oppressing me. I allowed it to go on too long. Once I took a stand, it did not immediately leave me. This evening when I had my juice, I immediately felt as if I was going to vomit. That sensation stayed with me well into the evening. I crawled up to bed about ten o'clock. On the way up, I almost broke my fast. I was extremely tempted. Praise the Lord, by His power; He sustained me in my hour of need.

WEDNESDAY MARCH 27, 2002—DAY THIRTY-NINE OF THE FAST
I awake afresh this morning unlike the previous day. Wow, unreal. I feel great physically as well as spiritually. Praise be His name. The oppression is gone. Hunger is still here, but the temptation has gone.

Much prayer has been sent forth. Much discipline has been accomplished. Much worship has been attained. Much spiritual strongholds have been pulled down. Much has been accomplished in the heavenlies.

Oh Lord, oh Lord, how majestic is your name. You are the Alpha and the Omega—the sustainer of all life; the giver and the taker. Father, I write now as the spirit is all over me; I am enveloped by your power flowing over me with the spiritual goose bumps from forehead to toes. Father, let me never forsake you.

THURSDAY MARCH 28, 2002—DAY FORTY OF THE FAST
Father, I come to you this fortieth day and praise you for sustaining me. I praise you for empowering me daily and minute by minute to fight

temptation. You have allowed me to fight the good fight. It was not easy, but you, God, ordained it, and therefore, so be it. Father, I thank you for revealing all that you revealed to me. Father, no one can ever put into words the blessings of this fast. You are awesome, and your mercies endure forever.

Father, anoint my preaching, Lord. Let it be your words that flow through my mouth, Lord. In closing, my Father, I would have never thought I would do another forty-day fast. Had it not been for my wife, I don't think I would have ever attempted it. Again, I thank you for my wife and thank you, Lord, for speaking through her.

Notes

Chapter 4

1. Ronnie W. Floyd, *The Power of Prayer and Fasting* (Nashville: Broadman & Holman Publishers, 1997), 35.

Chapter 6

2. Elmer L. Towns, *Fasting for Spiritual Breakthrough* (Ventura: Regal Publishing, 1996), 217.
3. Ibid., 218.

Chapter 7

4. Bill Bright, *The Transforming Power of Fasting and Prayer* (Orlando: New Life Publications, 1997), 43.

Chapter 8

5. Dave Williams, *The Miracle Results of Fasting* (Tulsa: Harrison House, 2004), 33.
6. John MacArthur, "MacArthur on Biblical Fasting," New-Testament-Christian.com, accessed on January 27, 2011, www.new-testament-christian.com/fasting.html.
7. Arthur Wallis, *God's Chosen Fast* (Fort Washington: CLC Publications, 1968), 12.
8. Towns, *Fasting for Spiritual Breakthrough*, 61.
9. Ibid., 200.
10. John MacArthur, "Fasting Without Hypocrisy, Part 1," New-Testament-Christian.com, accessed on January 27, 2011, www.new-testamnet-christian.com/fasting.
11. Towns, *Fasting for Spiritual Breakthrough*, 207–08.
12. John Piper, *A Hunger for God* (Wheaton: Crossways, 1997), 25.
13. Ibid., 52.

CHAPTER 9

14. Andrew Murray, Beliefnet Inc., accessed on July 7, 2016, www.beliefnet.com/Quotes/Evangelical/A/Andrew-Murray.

15. Bob Jordan, "Fasting." (paper, April 10, 1992).

16. Ibid.

17. Matthew Henry, *The New Matthew Henry Commentary*, ed. Martin H. Manser (Grand Rapids, Zondervan, 2010), 1060–61.

18. "Christian Fasting," AllAboutGod.com, accessed on January 27, 2011, www.allaboutgod.com/christian-fasting.htm.

CHAPTER 10

19. Stuart Scott, *From Pride to Humility* (Bemidji: Focus Publishing, 2002), 15.

20. "Biblical Fasting: What It Is and How to Do It," New Life Community Church, accessed on July 7, 2016, www.new-life.net/growth/other-articles/biblical-fasting.

21. Bright, *The Transforming Power of Fasting and Prayer*, 29.

22. Richard J. Foster, *Celebration of Discipline* (New York: HarperSanFrancisco, 1998), 47.

23. Ibid., 54.

CHAPTER 11

24. Hudson Taylor, Dailychristianquote.com, accessed on July 7, 2016, www.dailychristianquote.com/james-hudson-taylor-14.

25. Wallis, *God's Chosen Fast*, 36.

26. MacArthur, "MacArthur on Biblical Fasting."

27. Henry, *The New Matthew Henry Commentary*, 592.

28. Towns, *Fasting for Spiritual Breakthrough*, 27–28.

CHAPTER 12

29. Wallis, *God's Chosen Fast*, 9.

30. Ibid., 57.

31. Scott, *From Pride to Humility*, 2.

32. Ibid., 5.
33. "Biblical Fasting: What It Is and How to Do It."

CHAPTER 13

34. Towns, *Fasting for Spiritual Breakthrough*, 17.
35. Steve Walker, "Fasting," sermon, accessed on June 17, 2012.
36. Foster, *Celebration of Discipline*, 57–8.
37. Walker, *Fasting*.
38. Floyd, *The Power of Prayer and Fasting*, 4–5.
39. Ibid, 52–3.
40. Ibid, 56.
41. Lauren Daigle, Paul Mabury, and Michael Farren, "Trust in You," performed by Lauren Daigle, CentricSongs (Seasac) (Sony, ATV Timber Publishing, 2014), CD.

CHAPTER 14

42. Floyd, *The Power of Prayer and Fasting*, 4.

CHAPTER 15

43. John Wesley, oChristian.com, accessed on April 13, 2016, www. christian-quotes.ochristian.com/christian-quotes_ochristian. cgi?find=Christian-quotes-by-John+Wesley-on-Fasting.

CHAPTER 16

44. Piper, *A Hunger for God*, 124.

CHAPTER 17

45. Floyd, *The Power of Prayer and Fasting*, 7.
46. *Wikipedia*, "Got Milk?" accessed August 2, 2016, https://en.wikipedia. org/wiki/Got_Milk%3F.
47. Christopher and Angela Yuan, *Out of a Far Country* (Colorado Springs: Waterbrook Press, 2011), 19.
48. Ibid., 116.

49. Ibid.
50. Ibid.
51. Ibid., 71.
52. Ibid., 110.
53. Ibid., 147.
54. Ibid., 148.
55. Ibid., 186.
56. Ibid., 172.
57. Ibid., 191.

Chapter 18
58. Williams, *The Miracle Results of Fasting*, 30.
59. Yuan, *Out of a Far Country*, 110.
60. Williams, *The Miracle Results of Fasting*, 46–7.

Appendix
61. Natalie Nichols, "American Founders and Presidents: Proclamations for Public Fasting and Prayer," Shades of Grace Ministries, accessed July 14, 2016, www.shadesofgrace.org/2010/05/04/americas-founders-proclamations-for-fasting-and-prayer/.
62. William J. Federer, "When Our Leaders Used to Call Us to Prayer and Fasting," *WND*, accessed July 14, 2016, www.wnd.com/2010/07/174133/#!.
63. Ibid.
64. Natalie Nichols, "American Founders and Presidents: Proclamations for Public Fasting and Prayer,".
65. "Proclamation—Fasting Humiliation and Prayer—1795, Massachusetts," WallBuilders, accessed July 14, 2016, www.wallbuilders.com/libissuesarticles.asp?id=43.
66. "Proclamation—Humiliation Fasting and Prayer—1799" WallBuilders, accessed July 14, 2016, www.wallbuilders.com/libissuesarticles.asp?id=143595.

67. "Proclamation—Fasting Humiliation and Prayer—1807, Connecticut," WallBuilders, accessed July 14, 2016, www.wallbuilders.com/libissue-sarticles.asp?id=45.

68. "Proclamation—Humiliation Fasting and Prayer—1810" WallBuilders, accessed July 14, 2016, www.wallbuilders.com/libissuesarticles. asp?id=160882.

69. "Proclamation—Humiliation Fasting and Prayer—1815" WallBuilders, accessed July 14, 2016, www.wallbuilders.com/libissuesarticles. asp?id=160880.

70. "Proclamation—Humiliation Fasting and Prayer—1860" WallBuilders, accessed July 14, 2016, www.wallbuilders.com/libissuesarticles. asp?id=3587.

71. "Proclamation—Fasting Humiliation and Prayer—1863," WallBuilders, accessed July 14, 2016, www.wallbuilders.com/libissuesarticles. asp?id=131332.

72. Lawrence D. Jones, "Rick Perry Invites US Governors to 'Prayer and Fasting' Rally," *The Christian Post*, accessed July 14, 2016, www. christianpost.com/news/texas-gov-rick-perry-to-host-prayer-rally-to-solve-americas-problems-50897/.

73. "American Family Association Defends Louisiana Gov. Bobby Jindal's Prayer Rally at LSU: Prayer Is the Sole Purpose," *The Advocate*, accessed July 14, 2016, www.theadvocate.com/baton_rouge/news/ politics/article_8bacdb77-d80f-5fff-95c5-9d5744fa1b07.html.

74. Scott, *From Pride to Humility*, 5.

Bibliography

Books

Bright, Bill. *The Transforming Power of Fasting and Prayer.* Orlando: New Life Publications, 1997.

Floyd, Ronnie. W. *The Power of Prayer and Fasting.* Nashville: Broadman & Holman Publishers, 1997.

Foster, Richard J. *Celebration of Discipline.* New York: HarperSanFrancisco, 1998.

Henry, Matthew. *The New Matthew Henry Commentary.* Martin H. Manser, Ed. Grand Rapids: Zondervan, 2010.

Piper, John. *A Hunger for God.* Wheaton: Crossways, 1997.

Scott, Stuart. *From Pride to Humility.* Bemidji: Focus Publishing, 2002.

Towns, Elmer. L. *Fasting for Spiritual Breakthrough.* Ventura: Regal Publishing, 1996.

Wallis, Arthur. *God's Chosen Fast.* Fort Washington: CLC Publications, 1968.

Williams, Dave. *The Miracle Results of Fasting.* Tulsa: Harrison House, 2004.

Yuan, Christopher, and Angela Yuan. *Out of a Far Country.* Colorado Springs: Waterbrook Press, 2011.

Papers

Jordan, Bob. "Fasting," 1992.

Sermons

Walker, Steve. "Fasting," 2012.

Songs

Daigle, Lauren, Paul Mabury, and Michael Farren. "Trust in You." Performed by Lauren Daigle. CentricSongs (Seasac). Sony. ATV Timber Publishing, 2014. CD.

Websites
www.allaboutgod.com
www.beliefnet.com
www.christianpost.com
www.christian-quotes.ochristian.com
www.dailychristianquote.com
www.new-life.net
www.new-testament-christian.com
www.shadesofgrace.org
www.theadvocate.com
www.wallbuilders.com
www.webster-dictionary.net
www.wikipedia.org
www.wnd.com

Author Biography

As a former stockbroker, Gregory E. Von Tobel has been involved in full-time prison missionary work for more than a quarter of a century. He is the founder and president of Prisoners for Christ Outreach Ministries, (PFC) a ministry dedicated to taking the Gospel of Jesus Christ into the jails, prisons, and juvenile institutions not only in Washington State, but worldwide. PFC has field offices in thirteen foreign countries including Russia, Nepal, India, Kenya, Rwanda, Burundi, Congo, Uganda, Malawi, Ghana, Burkina Faso, Togo, and the Philippines.

PFC's volunteers worldwide conduct more than four hundred church services and Bible studies per month, averaging more than fourteen per day. PFC's national Bible Study Correspondence School has over twenty-six hundred inmates on its student body roster. Also, PFC's national inmate newspaper Yard Out is sent to over twelve hundred prison institutions nationally. In addition, PFC has over twelve hundred volunteers in the ministry worldwide in some capacity coming from over one hundred different churches.

Mr. Von Tobel was a former stockbroker of twelve years from 1978 through 1989 for various firms including Shearson Lehman Brothers and E.F. Hutton and Company when God called him into full-time prison ministry work. On May 14, 1990 God closed one chapter of his life and on the following day May 15, 1990 God opened up a whole new chapter. Greg has been ministering in Washington State Jails and Prisons for the last thirty-three years, six years on a volunteer basis and the last twenty-seven years as full-time missionary to those incarcerated.

Mr. Von Tobel has also served on the Governor's Panel of the Department of Corrections, Religious Services Advisory Council assisting the Department in setting religious policies and practices for inmates. In addition, he has served as past president of the Washington Chaplains Association and was a former Duvall City Councilmen.

Greg is married to Rhonda for the past forty years, and they have three children and three grandchildren.

Coming Soon!